BOMB
SHELTER

Center Point
Large Print

**This Large Print Book carries the
Seal of Approval of N.A.V.H.**

BOMB
SHELTER

Love, Time, and Other Explosives

MARY LAURA
PHILPOTT

CENTER POINT LARGE PRINT
THORNDIKE, MAINE

This Center Point Large Print edition
is published in the year 2022 by arrangement with
Atria Books, a division of Simon & Schuster, Inc.

Certain names and identifying details have been changed.

The text of this Large Print edition is unabridged.
In other aspects, this book may vary
from the original edition.
Printed in the United States of America
on permanent paper sourced using
environmentally responsible foresting methods.
Set in 16-point Times New Roman type.

ISBN: 978-1-63808-374-0

The Library of Congress has cataloged this record
under Library of Congress Control Number: 2022934601

To JP
To WC
To MG
Team Philpott Forever

In Brueghel's *Icarus*, for instance: how
  everything turns away
Quite leisurely from the disaster; the
  ploughman may
Have heard the splash, the forsaken cry,
But for him it was not an important
  failure; the sun shone
As it had to on the white legs
  disappearing into the green
Water; and the expensive delicate ship
  that must have seen
Something amazing, a boy falling out of
  the sky,
Had somewhere to get to and sailed
  calmly on.

W. H. Auden,
"Musée des Beaux Arts"

Life changes in the instant. You sit down
to dinner and life as you know it ends.

Joan Didion,
The Year of Magical Thinking

CONTENTS

PRELUDE

SHADOWS

I remember now standing with my face to the horizon in the waist-deep tide of the Gulf of Mexico, making up a dance routine. What's strange is that this memory was lost under a pile of other moments and more pressing daily calculations for decades; then, a couple of years ago, it floated right up to the surface, as clear as the water in the gulf.

At nine years old, I liked to imagine that I might one day command an audience in some sort of performance—not ballet, I was no good at it, but maybe some kind of pep rally like the big girls at my school were always having, or in a dance contest where most of the dancing was just walking and clapping and doing jazz hands. In the water, I was hard at work on choreography for "Stop! In the Name of Love," one of the songs my mother had sung along to on the oldies station as we drove down the highway from Tennessee to the Florida panhandle. We were on our annual beach trip with my grandmother, whom we'd picked up in Alabama.

Loud voices broke my concentration.

"Little girl!"

I turned around.

"Little girl!" a man's voice yelled again, but I

13

couldn't identify the source of the voice, because gathered on the shore were dozens of people, all bunched up at the water's edge. Everyone was shouting.

Was a girl in trouble? Was she breaking a rule? Or was everyone cheering for her? Had she done some kind of trick? I looked around the breakers on either side of me, searching for another person about my size, another girl in a stretchy nylon bathing suit with a worn, pilled bottom from sitting in the sand. Another girl with her elbow-length, sun-bleached hair tied up on top of her head in a bun that had been soaked in salt water, then dried, then soaked again, creating a nest of knots that would take an hour of combing to remove. The water had been full of children a second ago. Where were the other kids? Where was that little girl?

Had she gone under? I peered down and didn't see anyone swimming under the surface, no girl sneakily holding her nose to fool her parents into thinking she had disappeared. What I saw instead were empty trash bags, at least twenty of them. Black, floppy, as wide across as my own wingspan, the bags drifted through the water past my feet, pulled along by the current. Just beneath and behind them, their matching shadows floated across the sandy ocean floor.

That's littering. I thought of the owl in the public service announcement that was always interrupting Saturday morning television: "Give a hoot, don't pollute."

I began wading back toward the beach to find out what all the fuss was about. I lifted my knees high, careful to take big, marching steps, which I imagined would warn any crabs to scurry away before I stepped down. I didn't want to hurt any ocean animals. Also, I had seen on cartoons how crabs were always chomp-chomping their crab hands, and I didn't want them to hurt me either. I had never actually been pinched, but I still thought *crab* whenever the jagged edge of a broken shell nicked the raisined flesh of my foot.

Pokes and scrapes on my feet were part of going to the beach, just like the stinging rash that covered my skin. If you lined me up next to the rest of my family, I looked like the guest they had brought on vacation. Tanned to a deep brown within twenty-four hours of arrival, my mother and brother didn't have to bother with sunscreen, but I always burned crimson. (My dad, a doctor, had coloring closer to mine, but he usually stayed home to work.) All the sunblock products available at the time contained an ingredient that inflamed my skin; still, I swiped the SPF 15 stick across my cheeks every morning before we made the trek out to the sand. My mother encouraged me to reapply at lunchtime. It was either chemical burn or sunburn; at least the chemical burn meant we had tried.

Still, I loved the beach—the sea an endless swimming pool, the days so long you had to make up games to fill the time. I never wanted our beach week to end, no matter how many tangles, rashes, or cuts on my feet. The pain came with the territory, but the territory was so glorious that the pain didn't matter.

"Stop!" screamed a chorus of adult voices.

I froze where I stood in the water. And then I realized with a flash of hot embarrassment, as if I'd been caught stealing a piece of gum from my mom's purse, that they were all looking at me. Screaming at me.

I can feel that realization clicking into place all over again. *Oh.*

Surely and suddenly, I understood: The commotion was my fault. But how? Where was my brother, who had been playing next to me a moment ago? Where were my mom and my grandmother, who had just that morning unfolded two rusty metal and canvas lounge chairs to claim our family's plot in the sand?

Half the strangers on shore held up their hands at me like *stop in the name of love.* Others were sweeping their arms out and back, miming the motion of scooping me out of the water. Some were jabbing their fingers in the air. What were they saying? What had I done? What was I supposed to do?

16

I ran—or did the closest thing a child can do to running through moving water, high-stepping at double speed through the low waves to the hard-packed wet shore and into the softer white sand that gave way beneath my feet, slowing me down.

I didn't stop running until I found our chairs, where my brother stood open-mouthed and the adults sat up, craning their necks to look behind me. I fell into the sand by my grandmother, pressing my face into the towel draped over her shoulders. "What? What? What?"

"Look." She pointed to the water.

I lifted my face from the towel. To my relief, no one was looking at me anymore. Every beachgoer's face was aimed at the water and turning slowly to the right, watching the trash bags float by.

"Whoa!" my brother shouted.

Everyone but me must have heard the crowd's warning. Everyone but me must have seen them coming, a school of creatures known to be docile only as long as they're not provoked or stepped on. Everyone but me must have seen the barbed, poisonous tails whipping around my ankles as I danced and sang, unaware, in the shallow surf.

"I ran through stingrays," I whispered.

When I heard the words out loud, I began to cry so hard I could barely breathe.

PART ONE

HELLO FROM
UPSIDE DOWN

Three and a half decades after I crashed into the sand, I lay flat on my back on my living room rug.

I have two herniated discs in my upper spine, an injury caused not by swerving my car into a ravine to miss a deer or leaping bravely from a burning building with a blanket-wrapped child in my arms, but by spending too many hours for too many years hunched over a laptop. I know exactly what I'm supposed to do to take care of myself—the stretching and relaxation exercises I learned and continue to relearn at physical therapy, where posters on the wall cheer, "Movement is medicine!"—but I tend to default to what gets me through the day with fewer interruptions, which is instead to clench my neck and shoulders, overcompensating for my wobbly spinal column. As morning turns to afternoon, my shoulders crank up higher and higher. If I continue ignoring my body's signals to stop squeezing my muscles so tight, I'm exhausted by evening. It feels as if my neck can't hold the weight of my skull, like my head might roll right off my body.

That is why, late on a December evening, I was lying on the floor, trying to make up for everything I didn't do when I should have.

• • •

The house was quiet that night. Both teenagers had already shuffled off to bed. "G'night, Tarp!" my son had called to his sister, using the nickname that always made both of them laugh but that actually poked fun at me, not her. My daughter is allergic to grass and several kinds of pollen, and when her allergies flare up she gets wheezy and itchy. One morning while buttering the kids' toast, I had wondered aloud whether it was wise for her to sit on the ground at school when they had class outside. "Maybe you could bring something to put between you and the grass, like a towel or . . . a small tarp?" Both kids doubled over laughing. "Mom, everyone would call her Tarp Girl for the rest of her days!" my son had said. Now "Tarp" was shorthand for "beloved baby sister of funny big brother, and daughter to absurd mom."

I could just hear my husband, John, upstairs running water to brush his teeth. He must have been ready to pass out after a Sunday afternoon spent gamely performing every holiday task that popped into my head: haul the box of twinkly lights and decorations down a ladder from the attic, put it back up, wait, no, get it back down again.

I was glad everyone had ended the day in relatively decent spirits. Our evening had been tense. I had squabbled with my son about homework. We had eaten crummy takeout, because I had forgotten to plug in the slow cooker. Instead of brimming over with Christmas cheer, I had been short with everyone, irritated by a pileup of timely demands: figuring out presents for family, reminding the kids to clean up the notecards and paper they'd strewn everywhere while studying for exams, planning how to celebrate and where and with whom. We were all feeling bruised, but we were on our way to a night of rest and a new day.

As my knotted neck muscles began to let go just a bit and my shoulder blades melted toward the floor, I looked up at the Christmas tree and let a reel of holiday memories play in my mind: My first Christmas out of college in the apartment my roommate and I shared, where we threw a tree-trimming party so people would bring us ornaments. My first Christmas married to my college sweetheart, still in my early twenties, hanging an assortment of new trinkets John and I had received as wedding gifts on a skinny table-top shrub. My first pregnant Christmas, closer to thirty, when I couldn't sleep and wanted to gobble up every frosted snowflake cookie within reach.

The Christmas Day three years after that, when my newborn daughter and I came home from the hospital: John and I told our toddler son it was December twenty-fourth, because we wanted to have "Christmas Eve" as a family. I nursed the baby by the tree in our den, the lights making her appear to glow from within. I felt both sore and powerful as I fed her body from mine. Keeping her alive made me feel alive.

More Christmas memories: The year my son asked for a hammer and rocks, because he loved nothing more than cracking open geodes to look at their sparkling insides. The letters my daughter wrote to the North Pole, always beginning with a polite inquiry as to the reindeers' health. The years of endless crafts and sugar. Cupcakes, popcorn balls, peppermint bark. Good lord, the gingerbread houses—such hilariously grotesque wrecks of icing and gumdrops. They looked like what might happen if a tornado tore through the candy-colored village in a Dr. Seuss book.

More, more, more: The first time both kids slept past 7 a.m. on Christmas morning, two growing people who needed sleep more than they wanted to get up and demolish their stockings. The year my daughter asked, "So what's the deal with Santa?" I loved the Christmases when we stayed right here at home, our unit of four enjoying coffee and biscuits and hours upon uninterrupted hours in our bathrobes, but the years we had traveled to see the kids' grandparents were fun, too.

I thought about my parents, who were finally thriving again after a medical crisis that had given everyone a real scare the year before. I should call my mom and work out whether we were going to drive down to Georgia to see them before or after Christmas this year. I couldn't wait to hear the latest gossip from her garden club holiday luncheon. In terms of entertainment value, no reality show comes close to the scandalous highs and lows of a Southern women's garden club. To this day, my favorite episode is the tale of the meeting where the eighty-year-old grandes dames stormed out—*stormed* being a relative term, given that many of them used walkers—in protest of the "young members" (in their forties) using paper napkins instead of ironed linen.

I needed to ask her what to get my dad. A surgeon known as much for his meticulous skill in the operating room as for his colorful collection of ties, he spent his off-hours tinkering with tools in his basement and scouring Sam's Club for hot deals on bulk household goods. He could be hard to shop for, because he was, well, a tad quirky.

When I was in college—oh, this is one of my favorite Dad stories—he used to send the most bizarre care packages. Other kids received Tupperware containers full of homemade brownies, magazines, maybe a pair of mittens or an envelope of cash if they were lucky. That's what I got, too, if my mom was packing the box. But the packages from my dad almost never included a note and always contained canned food. It was a strange delight, toting those boxes across campus from the post office, knowing from their heft that they were filled with nonperishable items for a pantry I didn't have in my dorm room. Would it be single-serving cans of mixed fruit this time? Vienna sausages? Chef Boyardee ready-to-eat pasta meals?

It became a joke between my roommate and me. What would my dad send next? Did he think I didn't have access to food at school? That I might be building some sort of survival stockpile? We laughed every time one arrived—"Here we go, another bomb shelter box"—and stacked the cans under our beds. We ate the food, but not as fast as it accumulated.

Maybe I'd sign him up for a socks-of-the-month club. Had I ever done that before? I counted back through past holidays, memories of Decembers all stacked up like the last page ripped from every calendar.

I had been conscious, in some of those Christmas moments, of watching from some point in the future with a kind of pre-nostalgia. Now I was in that future. The accumulation of time hit me like a wave just then. *I am forty-four years old.* Could that be right?

When did I become this woman with nearly grown children? I looked at the pale blue curtains, the ones I picked out when we moved into this house, and thought, *Those are* grown-up *curtains. I paid for them with money I earned. I*

26

have a tax *spreadsheet.* A bright green rubber ball in the corner of the room caught my eye, and I thought, *Are John and I really on our fourth dog together? Do we really have just two Christmases left as a family under one roof before our son and then our daughter leave for college and holidays become "visits"?* Sometimes when I thought about the children leaving, I had a primal urge to swallow them whole, just absorb them back into my body and keep them with me forever.

If a man walking his dog on the street peered through our windows right then, he would see me lying there and think I was asleep. Or maybe, if he was the catastrophic sort, he would think I had fallen. He wouldn't understand that I was knocked flat not just by a cranky back but by both gratitude and fear. He couldn't know that I felt the universe had entrusted me with so much more than I could possibly keep safe.

He would not see the explosive vest I felt like I was wearing. Every joy, every loved one, every little thing I got attached to, every purpose I held dear—each one was another stick of dynamite, strapped to the rest.

The longer I lived, the more I loved, the larger this combustible bundle grew. I walked around constantly in awe of my good fortune and also aware that it could all blow up in an instant, flipping me head over heels into the air, vaporizing everything.

It's enough to make a person break down, the responsibility of it all. But it's also enough to make a person laugh, and that's what I did there on the floor, a gentle chuckle that became unstoppable giggling. What an utterly bonkers premise. Me, an adult, supposedly capable of caring for so much and so many. What a ludicrous miracle that I had kept these boats afloat, these people alive. But here we all were, just fine. Somehow, I was holding it together. "All you need is love," the old song went, and I guessed that was true. Love everyone hard enough, and they will be okay. Lie on the floor, and your backbone will realign itself.

I gazed up at the strange beauty of the inverted Christmas tree against the ceiling. Faceted glass balls reflected shards of light onto laminated paper ornaments made by the children years ago. Handprint angels did cartwheels across fir needles. The glittery gold star seemed to escape gravity, as if hovering in space. The scene tricked my brain, scrambling my proprioceptive senses into believing I, too, floated free and dizzy off the ground.

"Hello from upside down," I said to the quiet room.

Five hours later, at 4 o'clock in the morning, I heard a sound and sat upright in bed.

HURRY, HURRY

Imagine it's 4 a.m. and you hear something ramming down your front door.

No, that's not it—it's not the door. Your mind spins quick stories to explain the noise that has broken into your sleep. Has your dog somehow gotten into the bathroom and jumped into the shower, knocking over shampoo bottles and causing an unholy ruckus? You sit up, blinking in the dark, and say, "The door . . . ? The dog . . . ?" You can't make sense of the loud banging. The washing machine thumping off-balance with too many wet towels? No, it's not a machine sound, you start to realize as the rest of your senses catch up. It's a live sound. A personal sound.

Your spouse, also newly awake and confused, gets up and stumbles slowly, curiously, from the bedroom to the hall. Then his step abruptly changes.

He runs down the hall. You hear him yell a name, like a breath knocked out of his body by a punch. And then you jerk your legs from the blankets, and you run, too.

It is not a battering ram. It's not the dog. It's not a shampoo avalanche or a laundry overload. It is your son.

I should say: It is my son. I'm sorry. I'll take over the memory now. Just witness it with me, please.

It is my son. My first baby. He is not really a baby. He is about four-fifths of the way toward full-grown. He still goes to school and packs a snack, but he is also learning to drive. He's into environmental science. Point to any cloud and he can tell you what sort of weather it harbingers. He loves water—rivers, lakes, oceans—and has recently learned how to take apart the outboard motor of a boat and put it back together. If you saw his shape from afar, you would say, "There is a man." He has reached the age where he outgrows pants and shirts every three months or so. He is a teenager, which is half child and half brand-new adult and 100 percent fool-ass gooney bird who forgets to close the refrigerator after taking out the apple juice and drinking most of it. It is my boy on the bathroom floor.

I see his feet first.

"I feel a foot," my ob-gyn had said at my checkup when I was thirty-eight weeks pregnant. It's called footling breech when a baby is standing upright instead of curled up, head down, the way babies are supposed to be positioned before delivery. She tried, briefly, to turn him, pushing on my stomach with her hands, but he stood firm, resolute in his intention to kick his way out, which would have been fine if it didn't mean he would risk either breaking a limb or being strangled by the umbilical cord on his way. So my doctor scheduled a c-section, cutting him out of my body ten days before he was due. Better to break me than him.

Now he kicks his feet as if he's paddling, swimming desperately against some dreamworld riptide. The rest of his body is obscured by John, who kneels over him. I understand that our son's whole body is lifting off the floor with each kick. That's the sound I heard, his body slamming against the floor again and again and again.

It's amazing how much the human mind can do in a second or two, how fast the brain tries to impose order on something that doesn't make sense. It's as if there's someone in my head holding up flash cards, going, *Is this it? Is that it?* A floor, I know what that is. Feet, I know those. Bath mat, I see. But what is happening?

Then my brain flashes a card from twenty years ago—from my first job as a copywriter, when I wrote informational materials for a children's hospital. It's a pamphlet about seizures. What does it say?

> *Place something soft beneath the child's head.*
> *Do not put any objects in the child's mouth.*

*Clear the area of anything sharp or hard
that could harm the child.*

"Put the bath mat under his head," I say, calmly, quickly, as if I am in charge. John has already slid his hand under our son's head to absorb the impact. The noise has softened. Now it's the muffled *crack, crack, crack* of John's hand bones between skull and tile.

"Don't hold him down, but try to keep his arms and legs from hitting the tub so hard," I say. Who is speaking these words? Who am I? I am not myself. I am a hologram of a nurse, arrived on the scene to dole out instructions.

My son lies where he fell when he began to seize, just two steps into the bathroom when he dropped cold, his head now ricocheting against bathtub, toilet, and floor. His lips are purple, almost blue. He arches his feet involuntarily. Such big feet. He needs new shoes. I need to take him to the shoe store. No. I need to call for help.

I run back to the bedroom to pick up the phone. I see my fingers push the numbers.

The operator is composed, unflappable, just like me, the nurse hologram. She does not rush her words or strike a tone of alarm. We are two calm ladies having a tranquil chat, but while her voice stays even and smooth, mine just barely gives me away, shaking like I'm speaking into the whirring blades of a fan. She wants to know our address. She wants to know cross streets, so she can give the ambulance driver directions. Isn't there some kind of software that shows her this when the call comes in? This is why I ran back to our bedroom and called from the landline that we never use, that we had installed purely for emergency purposes—because I thought if you called 911 from a landline the operator would know where you were calling from, even if you couldn't talk. In my imagination, an emergency would leave me unable to speak. In this actual emergency, I am speaking. But the phone's stupid old-timey spiral cord has me tethered to a wall down the hall from my son, who cannot speak, who is not conscious at all as his body *slams, slams, slams* into the floor.

She wants to know how long he has been seizing. A minute, I think? Two? Maybe three. She wants to know about his breathing.

"Is he breathing?" I call out to John. He responds, yes, our son is breathing.

The operator says, "I need to know how fast. Say *now* every time he takes a breath."

"Say *now* when he breathes," I yell.

"Now," John yells back.

"Now," I repeat into the phone.

"Now."

"Now."

"Now."

"Now."

I don't want to interrupt, but I need to know if the ambulance has left yet. Is it coming? *Hurry, hurry. Please hurry.*

She asks me to go unlock the front door. I need to put down the phone. "Will you stay on the line?" I ask. She says, "Yes, ma'am." I say, "Yes, ma'am."

I run downstairs to unlock the door, then John and I switch places. He goes to pick up the phone. I take his place at our son's side.

The slamming has stopped.

My son stares at the bathtub a few inches from his face. For several seconds he is still, just breathing.

He reaches slowly with one arm for the side of the tub, tries to pull himself from the floor. When he was a toddler, he'd try to pull up to standing during his bath, to splash and dance on his little soft potato feet, and I would say, "No sirree, we sit down in the tub. It's slippery. You don't want to fall."

He pulls on the tub until he is sitting, half-upright on the floor. He tries to get his feet under him, to stand, but I put my arm around his shoulders to hold him there. I know he's in no shape to get up, and I also know I'm not strong enough to keep him down if he really wants to stand. His legs are longer than mine, more powerful, dark haired. Man legs. I say his name.

He looks from the tub to me and around the

room with wild eyes. He is lost. His mouth opens, and he wails.

"Hey, it's okay, you're okay," I say. "Do you know who I am?" This is the question that comes out first. Not *What happened?* Or *Are you okay?* Or *What hurts?* But *Do you know who I am?*

Tears spill over his eyelids and roll down his cheeks. His mouth is still stretched into wail shape, but now he makes no sound at all. He shakes his head. *No.*

"I'm Mama. Mama's here. I'm right here. Do you know who Mama is?"

He shakes his head again, eyes wide, mouth stretched open.

"It's okay, it's okay. Do you know who you are? Who are you?"

He stares at me, pulling at the tub with one arm and reaching over my shoulder with the other, as if to escape. He winces, and all the muscles in his face tense, as if he has heard a deafeningly loud noise. I repeat the question: *"Do you know who you are?"*

He shakes his head and the wailing begins again.

"It's okay. You're all right. I've got you."

When he was small, he used to do a spot-on impression of a siren. Sometimes I'd hear it in the kitchen or my bedroom and look out the front windows, certain I'd see blue lights flickering past. *Wha-ooo, wha-ooo, wha-ooo.* He loved to let loose with it in crowded parking lots, watching shoppers with their carts freeze and look around. It sounded so real, he was occasionally called in to do sound effects for school plays. The only person who consistently knew it was him was his little sister. She could tell the difference even from a block away. After he grew and his voice changed, he couldn't do it anymore.

"How about a hug. Do you want a hug?"

His wail has tapered off. Now it's just a whimper. He nods.

I wrap my arms around my son's muscular back. My son, who does not know who I am. Who does not know who he is. Who knows nothing right this second but that his whole battered body hurts and that nothing makes sense and that, yes, he wants a hug. As we wait for help to come, he bows his head to my shoulder and cries, deep hacking sobs.

The emergency medical technician who arrives at my side on the bathroom floor confirms that it appears to have been a seizure. After a brief evaluation, the enormous, bald, kind-eyed man carries my boy down our stairs with the gentleness of a father. He nods toward the side door of the ambulance waiting in our driveway and says, "Ma'am, you can enter that way." I climb, instead, straight up into the back from the loading door along with the stretcher, and he says, "That works, too."

When the EMT speaks to my son, he says "we," as in: "Hey buddy, we're gonna have some questions now, see how we're feeling. Can you tell me your name?" My son says something that is not his name but has the right vowel sound— *"aahhhhh"*—and the man says, "There we go. Now we know who we are, don't we?"

I understand that my son is coming back, but I still do not fully understand from where.

"All of this is normal," the man says, meeting my eyes over my son's stretcher. "In the postictal state, there's a lot of confusion."

A lot of confusion, it's normal.

FIRESTARTER

I lacked graceful motor skills as a child (as I do now), and I often felt like I didn't fit in with my ballet classmates. My favorite part of class was the waiting period before it started, when I got to sit on the dusty linoleum of the studio floor making hand shadows on the wall with my friends while our teacher cued up a piece of Tchaikovsky or Beethoven on the stereo. When it was time to begin on this particular day, my fellow students and I formed a line at the barre, a matching set of small humans wearing identical baby-pink leotards and tights. We did not yet know that we would be learning frappé, a move in which a dancer extends one foot out in a quick motion, the toes brushing the floor. Literally translated, the word means "to strike."

By way of introducing this concept to us, our teacher asked, "What would happen if you pulled a match slowly across a matchbox like this?" and dragged one finger across the palm of her other hand. She called on me.

I, an eight-year-old, answered, "It would . . . catch on fire?" What else does a match do?

Our teacher barked a scornful laugh and asked the question again, this time to the whole group. "Class, would a match catch fire if you dragged it like this?" She did the finger-match thing again.

"Nooooo," the class chimed in unison.

"Correct, ballerinas. A match only catches fire if you strike it quickly, like so!" This time, she dashed her finger hard and fast across her palm. "If you strike a match slowly, *nothing* happens."

Standing there in first position on the paper-thin soles of my slippers, I thought: (A) Well, that was a trick question. (B) If you don't want us to do it slowly, why all the talk about doing it slowly? And (C) As a child living in an age where "don't play with fire" is both a literal safety rule and a figurative expression for "don't mess around with danger," how would I know anything about the effects of speed on matches, and why would an adult choose the finer points of flame ignition as a metaphor for explaining anything to me? I may not have spelled it all out in exactly those words, but those were the thoughts that reddened my cheeks with indignation and humiliation. Knowing about matches wasn't dangerous. *Not* knowing about matches was dangerous.

By the time I outgrew those pink slippers, I still had not mastered how to turn out a perfect plié, but I had learned something important about myself: I didn't like to be unprepared when spontaneously tested. Forever after, long past the time when beginner ballet had become a distant memory, I'd watch for useful bits of information to sock away just in case. I never wanted to feel powerless or embarrassed because of something I didn't know.

The frustrating yet thrilling question of "What don't I know?" drove me straight to books. As a very young reader, I couldn't get enough magical realism. To me, it stood to reason that if it was useful to know about dangerous things, such as fire and matches, it could only be more useful to know about things that went beyond dangerous to downright mystical. I devoured novels about people who had ordinary, everyday lives except for one paranormal power. Of the supernatural skills I read about, I was most interested in telekinesis, the ability to move things with one's mind, as well as extrasensory perception—"ESP" or "the sixth sense" to those obsessed with it, as I was.

I knew some basic facts of the universe, like gravity, but when you haven't covered introductory physics yet in science class, there's still room to wonder. Telekinesis fit precisely into the crack between what was obvious (a penny tossed into the air would come back down) and what was definitely out of the question (if I spread my arms like wings, I could take flight). How could I be sure that if I really concentrated, I couldn't push a chair across the room with my brain? When I saw planes flying in the sky, I considered the possibility that I was keeping them in the air with my mind. As long as I willed them to stay aloft, they wouldn't crash.

(When you are a child who believes your brain can keep planes from crashing, it's imaginative and precocious. When you're an adult who thinks your own churning mind is what keeps everything safe, it's called anxious.)

I found a copy of Stephen King's *Firestarter* at my grandparents' house and flipped through it, skimming past every scene except the ones in which a girl lit fires with her mind. I studied those scenes closely. When the movie version came out and the ads for it were plastered everywhere, I examined the image of a young Drew Barrymore walking away from a blaze, her blond hair windblown and tangly just like mine. I went into my backyard and stared at the swing set, tensing the muscles around my mouth and eyes to make my intense stare match hers, thinking, *Am I doing it?* I never set off so much as a spark.

After a year or two of trying to incinerate objects with my hot gaze, I gave up and moved on from magical realism to just-plain-real realism. Given the freedom to spend my sandwich baggie of nickels and dimes at the Scholastic Book Fair on anything I wanted, I started buying books in which the characters died. That sounds grim, I know. It's not that I didn't have a jolly disposition as a kid—I did! I decorated my book bag with smiley face stickers and split Rice Krispies

Treats with my friends over joyfully rowdy lunches in the cafeteria. It is true that I often dug with a metal cereal spoon in the meadow near my house for desiccated animal bones, but it is also true that I put on upbeat puppet shows for my neighbors with the shiny white raccoon skulls I found. Death was a fascinating fact of life. It seemed both interesting and wise to learn the general territory: the warning signs, the ways it could happen, the aftermath.

I got *The Diary of Anne Frank* for Christmas in fourth grade and read it from cover to cover over that school holiday and again as soon as I finished it. I also received *Death Be Not Proud*, a memoir by a father whose teenage son died of a brain tumor. You have to hand it to my parents for acknowledging my fascination and meeting it head-on.

That same season, I read and reread *A Summer to Die*, Lois Lowry's first novel. It's about a pair of sisters, fifteen-year-old Molly, with golden curls and a cute cheerleading uniform, and thirteen-year-old Meg, a quiet, nerdy misfit who loves her sister but has always envied her, too. After Molly starts getting gruesome nosebleeds, she is diagnosed with leukemia, and, as the title indicates right there on the cover, she dies. Meg does not transform into a saintly and newly generous-of-heart sibling because of her sister's struggle. Rather, as Molly sickens, Meg feels both the overwhelming anticipatory grief of losing her and the selfish longings of a typical teenager. She loves Molly and also resents the time Molly's illness requires of their parents. Meg's duality felt real to me. I loved this book.

Maybe that's when I became an English major in training, when my future as a reader and storyteller was cemented. We learned in school about foreshadowing, a thrilling concept. A shadow that comes *before* something? A hint of what will happen? If you could pick up on all the foreshadowing around you, it was basically the same as having ESP! I began reading books not just to satisfy curiosity, but also to find hidden treasure. Reading became a scavenger hunt. Of course, sad books had the most foreshadowing; that's why it was called fore*shadowing* and not fore*sparkling*. It became harder and harder for a book to surprise me, so carefully did I study each chapter for hints: the ripped teddy bear that foreshadows the death of a pet, the rain puddle that foreshadows a deadly flood.

As an adult, I have bonded with friends who shared my childhood fondness for literary tragedy and I have also tried to make sense of it for those who find it strange. I explain that the reasons I read sad books then were not so different from why I read sad books today.

I looked directly at the sadness in books as a child because I was curious. Looking made me feel profound sorrow, and while I didn't enjoy sorrow itself, I was amazed to know the depth of it. The more I saw and heard of the real world, the more I came to suspect that there was sadness everywhere, and if I was going to live in this world, I should understand its scale and reach.

I am still drawn to what I don't understand, because I imagine that if I can understand more, I might better anticipate what happens in life. I'm old enough to know better, but it's tempting to think that if I can just find all the foreshadowing, then I will know: How does everything turn out?

PINWHEEL

Our day in the hospital started at breakneck speed. In a blur, my son was rolled out of the ambulance into the building and down a hall to a room, *one-two-three-LIFT* moved to a bed, his T-shirt pulled off, a green cotton gown tied onto him, a wristband snapped on his arm. He disappeared inside a circle of people in scrubs, and then, as they walked away with clipboards hanging from their hands, everything slowed down. While we waited for a neurologist, I had nothing to do but sit on a hard chair by his bed and look at him. He looked back at me from the hospital bed, the mattress cranked up so he could see me, a light blue blanket pulled up to his shoulders. He dozed, woke up, and drifted back to sleep. He still had bedhead, his dark hair—it had been toast colored and smooth when he was a baby but over time had thickened into a full mop of thick, wavy, almost-black brown—matted at the crown like it always is at the breakfast table. But instead of eating his morning cereal, he was lying tucked into a blue cocoon in a yellow room, everything the color of sunshine and sky, ocean and sand.

From a hook on the wall hung a laminated card showing the illustrated pain scale. Say what you will for magnetic resonance imaging and laser-guided surgery, but to me, this illustration represents one of the greatest advances in modern medicine, even though it's nothing more than a cartoon panel of human faces. To communicate your discomfort, you need only point to the face that matches how you feel—from the broad smile of "No Hurt," through "Hurts a Little Bit" and "Hurts a Little More," all the way to the steep frown and teardrops of "Hurts the Worst." You don't have to speak the same language as your caretaker or even speak any language at all. You point to a simple picture, and just like that, you're understood. What a precious gift, that shorthand.

When I noticed my son's gaze had drifted to the pain scale, I asked, "Do you feel like any of those?"

I wanted him to choose the smiley face. I wanted him to be free of pain. I also wanted the doctors to listen and take his case seriously, so I wondered if maybe it would be better if he chose the slightly-less-happy face. Not the frown-and-tears face, though, please not that. Mostly I wanted answers to questions such as, "What happened?" "Why?" "When will it happen again?" "How can we stop it?" And another question, unspoken: *Is there any way to transfer whatever's happening to him to me instead?*

He pulled his arm from the blanket. Then he

stuck out his finger, hesitated, and pointed . . . to the doorknob. He fell back asleep.

The first neurologist who visited our room stood at the foot of my son's bed and said, well, a single seizure could be anything. A one-off, a quirk. Best to leave it alone and hope he doesn't have another one. You wouldn't want to start treating him with anti-seizure medication unless absolutely necessary. Those drugs are no joke. They have all kinds of side effects. Plus, plenty of kids have one seizure and never have one again. It could have been a weird bug. There's no reason to assume it's anything serious. No reason to assume it's, say, epilepsy.

I hadn't yet assumed anything.

Later, John told me one of the paramedics asked if our son might have been on drugs. It took John by surprise, but it's a fair question, I guess. Our son was in tenth grade, and his peers had begun experimenting. Vaping was all the rage, and kids were inhaling poisonous fumes through pipes made to look like school supplies. What appeared to be a mechanical pencil might actually be a delivery device for an addictive, fruit-flavored mixture containing chemicals that shredded human lung tissue. (Every time I think about the fact that adults at some company sat around a table coming up with ways to market that shit to children, I wish for the superpower to teleport myself into the room and torque their balls until they scream for mercy and swear to reform their predatory ways, but that is a rant for another time.) While I had been riding in the ambulance, John—who had stayed behind with our daughter so he could get her to school and then come join me at the hospital—had gone into our son's room and dumped the contents of his backpack onto his bed, pulling out every pen and taking it apart. He stuck a USB thumb drive in his mouth and tried to suck air through it. Nothing.

The only possible cause I had briefly considered during the ambulance ride was a brain tumor. After I left my job at the children's hospital two decades ago, I had worked for the American Cancer Society, the aftereffect of which was that I had a lot of spare, outdated cancer knowledge filed away in my head. I couldn't remember what I had learned about brain tumors, other than that seizures could be a symptom and that some tumors were survivable and others amounted to a death sentence. I did not let my thoughts linger there for long.

I knew just enough to know how much I didn't know—and that knowing a little more could make a big difference. I knew that seizures happen when there's a surge of electricity in the brain. It seemed useful to know whether you had experienced a random bolt of lightning or if you should expect a recurring storm.

Before the neurologist left our room, I asked if she would be kind enough to wait with us just a minute while I texted my sister-in-law. I realized it must make doctors nuts to deal with parents tethered to their phones, but my brother's wife also happens to be a pediatric neurologist. To dial her in would be like having a second team member in the room, and I wanted her opinion. So while the doctor waited, I typed out a quick update and told my sister-in-law that the exam thus far had been inconclusive. It looked like we might be sent home without a diagnosis.

She wrote back: *Ask for an EEG. Bar the door and say you won't leave until you have it.*

I told the doctor we would stay until we knew what we were dealing with.

John likes to share the story of a job interview he had when he was a teenager. The hiring manager asked, "If you were a fruit or vegetable, what kind would you be?"

He answered: a cantaloupe. Every time he tells it, I am so impressed by the sureness of his response, that when asked about his alternate existence as produce he could picture it immediately. A cantaloupe, obviously. Because it's plain on the outside but flavorful and interesting if you're able to access its inside. Absolutely.

When I think about that question, I struggle

to narrow down an answer. A single fruit or vegetable to represent my whole essence? I guess if I had to pick, I'd say grapefruit. Grapefruits look a lot like their cousins, oranges, but their flavors are more dynamic. They taste sour and sweet but also bitter, not so simply sugary. Even the name doesn't stick to one lane. *Grape*fruit, for a fruit that's not a grape? I like the whimsical complexity.

The great thing about "What kind of ____ would you be?" quizzes is that they do all the work of sorting you out according to the answers you give, and that's why I take them all the time. Just respond to some basic questions, and instantly get a diagnosis as to which type or category or Avenger or Golden Girl you are. Then whenever you face a challenge in life, you can ask yourself, "What would Thor do?" You can even use the knowledge retroactively. Let's say you've been replaying a past incident in your head, going over it again and again, wondering if it could have gone differently. When you find out you're a Dorothy, you can say, "Ah yes, I acted in accordance with my inner Dorothy-ness. It was inevitable." Retrofitting destiny over your behavior isn't an airtight strategy for mental peace if you think about it too hard, but if you let yourself believe, you can give yourself temporary salvation from the existential abyss. That's why these quizzes are so popular.

A few years ago, when I worked in bookstore marketing, I was at a banquet and the table talk turned to personality types. "What would your Spice Girls name be?" asked the woman seated next to me.

"You mean, like . . . Book Spice?" I asked.

"Too obvious," she said. Fair enough. There's nothing revelatory about a Spice name that just states your job. That would be like calling an astronaut Space Spice. "It has to say something about who you really are," she said. I mulled it over as I picked the celery out of my salad. I'll tell you right now what vegetable I would *not* be: celery.

I actually took an online quiz once to find out which of the Spice Girls I was most like. I got Baby Spice, which bothered me, so I took another Spice Girls quiz from a different source to see if I could get a different answer. On the second quiz, I got Baby Spice again. I started to take a third test, but I quit before I got to the "calculate results" button. I know it doesn't *really* mean anything, the Baby Spice thing, but a triple score would start to look significant. Am I somehow deeply, essentially Baby Spicy? Better not to know.

That's fair, by the way, taking a test more than once. I've taken the Myers-Briggs test, decided I don't like the result, and taken it again with different responses. It's not like I'm lying. Lots of answers can be true answers. Sometimes I'm a thinker and sometimes I'm a feeler. At a party, am I more likely to stick close to the wall or venture to the center of the crowd? Depends on who's at the party, whether I'm tired, and where the bar is. Today I'm an INTJ, but tomorrow I might be ESTJ. And if I'm trying to make the case that I'm an INTP, I can take the test again and again until it gives in and tells me I am one. Same with the Enneagram. I'm usually a type one, but with a few tweaks to my answers I can be a type three.

I took another online personality test once that claimed to be able to rank a person's most prevalent traits. Two traits showed up tied in first place for me—anxiety and cheerfulness. I don't know if I've ever felt so validated. Am I here to tell you we're all going to die? Yes. Am I here to give you a pep talk along the way? Also yes!

I shouldn't have needed a test to tell me that about myself, though. Look at nearly any moment in my life, and there they are, irrational cheeriness and bone-crushing anxiety, skipping along holding hands. To wit: the first time I tried marijuana (out of a grand total of two times, both as an adult, because I'd been too afraid to touch any kind of drug in college). Sitting around a table on the back porch of a friend's mountain house as my special cookie kicked in, I got the chuckles. My hands were funny. My sunglasses were funny. My sandwich was *hilarious*.

A comedy of merriment played out before me! My abs began to ache from nonstop laughing. Tears ran down my cheeks. I tried to tell my friends how funny everything was—how funny *they* were!—but I couldn't speak. And then I thought, *What if I can't get enough oxygen because I'm laughing so hard? What if I choke?* If you're looking to prove the coexistence of cheer and anxiousness, the question "Could I die laughing?" really sums it up.

So that test, like the rest, told me only what I already knew. I didn't love it for its revelations; I loved it for the confirmation. It was soothing. Instead of wondering, *Am I weird for being this way?* I could say, ah, my way of being is a *known* way of being. It's a category. A code. It's something. I'm something.

Back at the work dinner, I thought about my tablemate's question as I pushed bits of celery toward the rim of my plate with my fork. Deep down, what am I about? What's my thing? I am a person who trusts data and loves information and feels soothed by sorting things. I'm a person who sees cause for delight everywhere but can't stop noticing danger everywhere, too, and who often struggles to reconcile the two. I'm a person who takes every personality test despite knowing her own personality very well, and then retakes them until she gets the label she wants.

"I'm Control Spice," I said.

$$\bullet \ \bullet \ \bullet$$

When it was time for the EEG—the electro-encephalogram that would measure electrical activity in my son's brain and render it as waves on a screen—a young technician wheeled in a machine on a cart. He parted my son's hair carefully, kindly, as he nestled the sticky round electrodes against his scalp and wrapped his head to hold the corresponding wires in place. Around and around he unspooled a ball of white gauze, covering my son's hair from forehead to nape, with a final pass under his chin to form a strap. Then he handed the mummy-wrapped patient a red and pink pinwheel on a yellow stick.

My son took the pinwheel in his hand and glanced at me, perplexed. I, equally bewildered, looked to the technician. What was this, some kind of party favor?

"Oh," he said, "first we're going to see what happens during hyperventilation."

He explained that the easiest way to get a child to re-create the drop in carbon dioxide that occurs when the body hyperventilates is to tell them to *blow, blow, blow* enough to keep a pinwheel moving.

I have always loved pinwheels. When I was little, it was such a score to talk my mom into adding a few extra cents to our grocery receipt so my brother and I could each pull a metallic flower from a bin by the checkout counter. I loved how if I puffed hard enough on the petals, the red-blue-red-blue-red-blue spun into mesmerizing violet. Nowadays when I see a pinwheel, I still think of that simple, breathless childhood glee, but I also think of standing just inside the door of a hospital room watching a boy with tired eyes blow obediently on a dime-store trinket.

(Now that I think about it, I wish someone would ask, "If you were a toy, what would you be?" because I have an answer! I'd be a pinwheel.)

When the pinwheel test was over, the technician took it back and turned off the overhead light in the room. As he switched on a strobe bulb attached to his cart, he said, "This one's easy. You don't have to do anything, just rest." My son nodded and looked drowsily at the floor while the strobe began to flash.

Together in the darkened room, we were illuminated one split second at a time by a flickering light reminiscent of a haunted house or a dance club: my son in his bed, the technician at the machine, and me, trying to stay out of the way. I slipped my phone from my pocket and took a video of the line spiking up and down across the monitor. After the technician turned off the strobe and wheeled his machine out to the hall, I sent the video to my sister-in-law.

She texted back: *There it is.* So I knew before anyone came back to talk to us that there was something to see on that EEG.

Another half hour crawled by before a new doctor and his residents came in, lined up, and introduced themselves. The doctor segued so smoothly from his own name to the name of what had hold of my son's body, I didn't register what I was hearing until he was a few sentences along.

"Wait. What?"

"Juvenile Myoclonic Epilepsy," he said. "JME."

It's strange how a before-and-after moment can be so unceremonious.

"It's kind of a misnomer, though, because you don't have it only when you're a juvenile. You show your first symptoms as a teenager, but you have it for the rest of your life. Anyway . . ." the doctor said, and brushed his hands together as if he were finishing up lunch, "it responds very well to medication. A nurse will be by shortly with a prescription, and you can get it filled today on your way home."

I wanted to go home, but I also didn't understand how I was expected to know what to do when I got there. I thought, *Hold up. Is the medication that works so well the same medication someone told us earlier had all sorts of side effects? What are they? Who will check on us? How do we know if the drugs are working? You just met me. How do you know I can handle this?*

What I actually asked was, "When he goes to

bed tonight, should I put a gate at the top of the stairs?"

"No, no, nothing like that. Just let him rest. You'll need to set up a neurology appointment in a month or so." *Or so.*

Someone brought me a pile of papers to sign. Someone else brought a sample-size bottle of baby shampoo for washing off the leftover electrode glue. Everything they handed me I shoved into my purse, next to my wallet and my keys, to deal with later.

TURTLES, TURTLES, TURTLES

We live in an old, wooded Nashville neighborhood, a few blocks from three thousand acres of parkland. Rabbits, skunks, turkeys, and deer frequent the area, not to mention smaller creatures, such as lizard-quick iridescent skinks, rocklike clusters of gray snails, and little brown eastern box turtles—the official reptile of Tennessee.

I try to respect their wildness rather than treat them like the cast of a Disney movie. I would never try to capture any of these animals to make them live inside my house or wear tiny sweaters. Do I talk to them? Sure. We all do. One drizzly morning when my son was in middle school and had been learning French, I heard him outside saying, "Bonjour, mes amis les escargots. I bet you like that rain, don't you?" We don't feed the mammals, because teaching them to approach humans for food can have dangerous consequences, although I do occasionally—only occasionally, I swear—leave out a bit of leftover salad for the reptiles who like veggies. I put out a dish of fresh water on hot days, too, although I've noticed the smaller animals use it more as a splash pool than a drinking pond. And, okay,

I have also named them sometimes, at least the recurring visitors.

Shortly after we moved into the house, we noticed box turtles of various sizes often made their slow way across our backyard, temporarily pressing the grass and weeds into turtle prints as they went. From afar, it looked like an invisible person was shuffling by, their steps mashing the ground cover flat. You could only see the turtles if you got close and looked directly down.

For several years, one turtle made a habit of wandering onto our back porch. I always knew he was out and about when I heard one of the kids say, "Oh, hey, Frank." We figured he must live somewhere around the perimeter of our house; he wasn't just passing through.

One morning I heard a *knock, knock, knock* on the front door, but when I looked out the window I saw no one. It happened again a few minutes later. The third time, I yanked the door open and stood confused for a moment until I looked down. There was Frank, standing on the doormat.

It soon became a regular occurrence. Once we knew it wasn't a burglar or an obnoxious ring-and-run jokester, we didn't mind, although we worried that Frank might hurt himself, banging his head against the door like that. Every time it happened, we picked him up and moved him to a shady spot. Frank's pranks, as we dubbed them, became a problem only when Frank started knocking in the middle of the night. One morning I woke to John sitting up, rubbing his eyes.

"What's wrong?" I asked.

"I didn't sleep all night," he said. "I had to keep moving Frank."

Later that morning, I heard a scuffle out front and opened the door. "Well, well, well," I said. "Look who it is." This time, Frank took a few steps into the house, peering around. I lifted him up carefully and relocated him to the yard.

Like all humans, my mind is wired to look for the story in any situation. Where's the beginning, the middle, the twist, the end? And what's the moral? You could spin all sorts of theories as to why Frank started knocking—from the tragic (in which he's the abandoned pet of our home's former owners), to the *Poltergeist* (in which the house was built on a turtle burying ground), to the practical (in which he's begging for food). The bottom of our door had a shiny brass kickplate affixed to it, and because Frank was only about four inches tall, it probably functioned as a big looking glass to him. We guessed he was picking a fight with his own reflection. If I wanted to, I could weave a parable about how everyone's fighting an inner monster. Like Frank, we all have an enemy in the mirror, and our greatest danger is that we could destroy ourselves while battling it.

Several weeks into Frank's pranks, my husband shook my shoulder at 6 a.m. "Come see." This time when we opened the door, we saw someone new.

This turtle was a bit smaller, slightly more vividly colored. "That's a different turtle, right?" he said. We couldn't figure out whether it was male or female, so I googled "how to sex turtles" (a search phrase that, in retrospect, could have gone terribly wrong). Turns out, there are signs—subtle differences in shell shape and eye color—but most people can't tell for sure without the help of a vet. I wasn't going to subject this turtle to a veterinary examination, and I certainly wasn't going to pressure my new friend on gender identity. We named this one Fancy.

Fancy showed up several days in a row but never knocked, only stood quietly before the door's shiny surface. When we opened it, Fancy froze, then slowly turned and walked back into the bushes, as if we'd both agreed to look away and pretend the encounter hadn't happened.

I imagined that Fancy just wanted to gaze at their reflection to better know themselves. Who among us hasn't wondered, *What am I to others?* We feel you, Fancy.

One day, as I watched Fancy nibble grass, I began to doubt our theory that Frank and Fancy were two different turtles. I pulled up pictures I'd taken of each.

"I think Frank and Fancy might be one and the same," I told my husband. "We never see them together, and they both have this handprint marking on their backs." Perhaps Frank was a much more complex individual than we first suspected. Who isn't?

"Nope," he disagreed. "Different turtles." Over the next few weeks, we stopped seeing Fancy, if we had ever seen Fancy at all. Only Frank.

I put out some cherry tomatoes, spinach, and a dish of water one morning. The cherry tomatoes disappeared fast. No one ate the spinach.

Proverbs about the transitory nature of life say we don't inherit the earth from our ancestors but borrow it from our children. They say we're only borrowing our children, too, that they are on loan to us from wherever they came from and wherever they are going. Same with turtles, I suppose. I'm just the borrower.

This wasn't the first time turtles had played a part in our family's lore. When my son was in preschool, he learned the "I Have a Little Dreidel" song but mispronounced "dreidel" as "turtle." He mangled the lyrics until it became a whole different song, a rhyme he asked us to sing each night:

Turtles, turtles, turtles
How I love you so

Turtles, turtles, turtles
Never let you go

It was our bedtime routine for a decade.

I could read my turtle visits as a sign from the universe that my role as a parent was changing. My children would be finished with high school in a flash. College and adulthood weren't so far off in the future. I would not be able to protect them forever, and I had to face it.

Turtles, turtles, turtles . . . *time to let them go?*

Or I could look at myself in the mirror and sternly say, *no,* the universe doesn't know about that song and is definitely not sending me a sign. Just because I lie awake at night wondering, *What's going to happen?* doesn't mean everything I see by daylight is a possible answer.

The nursery song I sang to my baby—"never let you go"—had been a lie. But it wasn't a cruel lie. It was a hopeful one. It was a lie to me as much as to him. It was a loving work of fiction to let myself enjoy those warm, snuggly evenings without thinking about the fact that one of those times would be the last time.

So. You see what happens when I just try to tell a nice story about a turtle.

Can you blame me, though? Assigning meaning to events is so satisfying. I want themes, threads, a plot that begins with a question and then proceeds toward resolution. I want people to learn their lessons and change their ways and for the moral of every story to make us better as a species. But look at the news—full of arbitrary injustices and disasters, human beings treating one another, themselves, and the earth with callousness. I want the world to conform to a story that makes sense, but that desire crashes against the rock of reality again and again. My soul sometimes feels as battered as Frank's head must after banging on my door.

The phrase "turtles all the way down" refers to the "world turtle theory"—derived from various Hindu, Chinese, and Native American myths—that the earth is actually flat and sits balanced on a turtle, who is balanced on another turtle, who is balanced on another, et cetera. It's a way of saying there ultimately isn't any real truth, because everything we take as fact is explained by another fact, which is validated by another fact, all the way down to some kind of fact we had to have made up in the first place. Our whole lives, by that logic, rest upon explanations we've rigged up to justify explanations for whatever we were looking to understand. Turtles upon turtles upon turtles.

I think the turtle theory is a weird answer to the question *Is there any truth?*—but then again, look at me. I keep trying to make sense of my life by stacking stories upon stories upon stories. Who am I to judge?

As the cold of deep winter settled in, we stopped hearing Frank rattle his splashing dish on the front porch. We did some more research and learned that turtles bury their bodies under piles of leaves and dirt to stay warm in the winter. We knew it would be months before we saw him again.

Maybe the turtles knocked to suggest I stop trying to understand and explain everything. Perhaps they came to let me know that nature—including human nature—won't conform to storytelling conventions, no matter how much mental energy I spend trying to make it. They might have come to say, *Look! The world is full of spontaneous gifts you can't control or rationalize.*

But probably not.

They came and went—they come and go still—for reasons of their own. They're turtles. It's not their job to teach me anything.

ONE MIGHT WONDER

I didn't know until the days immediately following my son's seizure, in which I spent many hours doing online research, that epilepsy isn't a disease. It's a term used to mean "has seizures." A neurological syndrome that causes seizures is called epilepsy, even if it works quite differently from another neurological syndrome that causes seizures and is also called epilepsy. It's an even wider catchall category than "cancer." One person with one kind of epilepsy and another person with another kind may live very different lives. The terminology is constantly evolving as we learn more about how the brain works. I'll tell you right now, I'm probably not getting it 100 percent right here, but scientists don't yet have it completely figured out either.

It's a wily foe, epilepsy. It can threaten to take down your loved ones, but you can't predict exactly when or where or how. Treating it involves a lot of guesswork.

Depending on the type of epilepsy—or seizure disorder—a person has, they may have different types and frequency of seizures. Some babies have seizures and then outgrow them. Some people start having seizures later in life.

Most people who haven't actually seen someone have a seizure picture a certain kind of thing when they imagine one—probably a scene from a movie, in which someone falls to the ground and flops around like a fish. That used to be called a grand mal seizure, but it's called a generalized tonic-clonic seizure, or GTCS, these days (at least until someone changes the term again). This is the type of seizure my son had that morning.

In generalized seizures, the electricity hits both brain hemispheres at once. "Focal" seizures look different depending on which lobe of the brain gets hit with the extra electricity; often in a focal seizure, a person remains partially conscious but gets really confused. A person may have only one of these types of seizures, or they may have multiple different kinds of seizures at different times. The combinations, as they say at Applebee's, are endless.

Then there are myoclonic seizures, which you've probably witnessed before without even realizing. They're harmless and extremely brief. In a myoclonic seizure, a person has a single, quick muscle twitch, usually in one limb or sometimes in the neck or another area of the body. If you had a myoclonic seizure in your arm while eating a salad, it might just look like you yanked your fork a bit to the left and flung a bite of lettuce on the table. If you've ever dreamed about falling and felt your body jerk for a second—that's similar to the sort of movement that happens in a myoclonic seizure. Triggers for both myoclonic seizures and generalized tonic-clonic seizures in people with JME may include stress, sleep deprivation, and bright, flashing light.

Oh, and there's another fascinating type of seizure called an absence seizure. Out loud, you pronounce it the French way—"ab-sonce"—but when I see it in writing I hear it in my head as the English word *absence,* as in being absent, which makes perfect sense to me, because the way this seizure works, the person is there, but they're not *there.* In an absence seizure, a person has a brief lapse in consciousness. They might be sitting in class or having a conversation, and then all of a sudden they're staring off into space or blinking. Their teachers may describe them as "having difficulty concentrating" or "spacing out." Kids who have this kind of seizure often go undiagnosed for years.

If a kid like that spaced out at the dinner table and his blinks were long enough that he appeared to be sitting there with his eyes closed, a parent might think the kid is just having wacky table manners.

A parent might spend a decade wondering what her six-year-old meant when he told her, "I miss you when I blink."

A parent might realize then, after ten years, that when he blinked he was absent.

A parent might finally understand that, whether he fully knew it or not at the time, her child had been telling her something very important.

She might wonder, *Should I have known?*

EVERYBODY HAS SOMETHING

On our first visit to the upper floors of the children's hospital, one month after our trip to the emergency room, we met my son's new neurologist. Over the past few weeks, we had spoken as a family often about the upcoming appointment, holding on to our questions as patiently as we could until the time came. We knew little about what would happen at this meeting; in fact, all we knew was the name of the doctor, which we incanted with hope. Before we ever met him, we started calling him by his full name in conversation at home, including the suffix *MD*. Sometimes we just called him MD for short.

It wouldn't be quite correct to say I loved MD instantly, because *love* is the wrong word for a stranger and *instantly* is always an exaggeration when it comes to such things, but this would be accurate: In the span of an hour, I came to trust him in the rare way one can fully trust someone else with their child. I knew from looking him up online before our appointment that he was roughly my own age, but his open face, compact frame, and energetic gait as he bounded into the room in a white coat that hung almost to his knees gave him a boyish quality. When my son got up to greet him, the patient stood a good six inches taller than the doctor, who looked up and joked that his own young son was on track to outpace him in height, too. They sat back down, my son on the exam bench and his doctor on a wheeled chair, which he drove around the room with his feet, Flintstone-style, back and forth from the computer, where he took notes, and over to my son, where he sat eye to eye and listened.

As fleeting as our interactions had been with the emergency room doctors, our time with MD felt unhurried, even relaxed. My son told him how he was having difficulty sleeping, because, ironically, he was so anxious about getting enough rest, afraid with every passing minute that if he didn't fall asleep soon he would risk having another seizure. MD raised his eyebrows in affirmation: "Yeah, yeah, I get that." They talked some more, and then MD turned to me and asked, "What questions do you have?"

I flipped through my pocket-size spiral note-book, which I had filled with scribbled notes. I wanted to know more about my son's medication. He had been ramping up slowly over the past four weeks to a full dose of the drug he was prescribed in the emergency room. The doctors there had warned that although it was often difficult to find the treatment that worked best for each patient, "many types of epilepsy can be controlled with medication."

That's a sentence that on the surface is true, but which also conceals the complexity of its truth. It's kind of like "People are different" or "The electoral college system is complicated." One medicine that prevents seizures almost completely in many patients also can cause birth defects if women take it in their childbearing years. Another medicine controls seizures very well although it can also cause white-hot rage. Others do their job perfectly, except for the fact that they impair the body's ability to do its other jobs, such as sleeping, thinking, or digesting food. Still, it's true: Many types of epilepsy can be controlled with medication.

"How will we know if this is the right medicine?" I asked.

MD smiled, almost apologetically. "It can be a process of trial and error," he said.

Everybody has something. That's one of the things John and I began saying to the kids. We meant it as a way of normalizing what our son was going through—like, hey, nobody's without some medical adventure. Having a body means taking care of yourself in all the usual ways, plus whatever extra way might be required by your particular thing. You go to the doctor. You take your medicine. You do what needs doing, so you can go on with your life.

For example, here in our household, our daughter has asthma. One of our dogs has an eating disorder, and the other has chronic pancreatitis. And I have migraines. I don't spend much time thinking about my migraines these days, but when I first started having killer headaches in my early twenties I had to learn how to deal with them. The first medicine I tried gave me such strong heart palpitations that I called my dad, just to make sure there was no chance I was having a heart attack. (There are few stupider questions to ask over the phone than, "Do you think I'm having a heart attack?" The person on the other end of the line cannot possibly evaluate your cardiac condition based on your voice. Dad said, "I think it's probably fine.") I switched medications after that, and again after that. Eventually, I settled on a treatment that works without weird side effects. I still have migraines, but other than popping a pill and hanging out in a dark room for a while, there's not much I can do about them.

John's thing is Graves' disease. Early in our marriage, he developed this fairly common autoimmune condition in which his thyroid gland went into overdrive. The first indication was the startling amount of weight he lost in a short time—fifty pounds in a couple of months. Weight loss like that is something you don't notice and don't notice and don't notice and then *whoa,* you look over and see that your husband's blue-checkered button-down shirt fits like a parachute around him, loose and empty, crimped at the bottom where it's gathered into his pants, which are cinched closed by a belt on its tightest setting. Then you look back up at his face and go, "Holy shit, have you always had those cheekbones?" Food went right through him. Nothing stuck to his ribs.

Stranger, and maybe worse, his personality began to change. Again, it's the kind of thing you don't notice until you do. One day you realize that your smiley, agreeable loved one has a constantly furrowed brow. He slams doors. He spills a drop of wine on the sofa and yells, "It's ruined!"

And then the forgetfulness started. This was easy to notice, because as family members of anyone with memory loss will tell you, forgetting leaves evidence everywhere. On more than one occasion, John fed our dogs, put their bowls away, and got the bowls back down twenty minutes later.

"What are you doing?" I'd ask.

"Feeding the dogs," he'd say.

The dogs, as if complicit in the plan to get double dinners, said nothing.

This was during the time when I worked in

communications for the national office of the American Cancer Society. It was my job to present complicated medical information in a way that the public could understand. We'd been busy that year with a campaign to raise public awareness of colon cancer, one of the most unnecessarily deadly cancers.

I can confidently say that the person who became the most aware of colon cancer during the awareness campaign was me, the woman writing the awareness materials. When all John's symptoms became suddenly obvious—the weight loss, erratic behavior, loss of memory—I knew what I was looking at. My husband definitely had colon cancer, and it had absolutely metastasized to his brain. His eyes were bugged out and puffy, too. Clearly, the tumor was pressing on them from within his skull.

I might have been embarrassed about mis-diagnosing my husband with a brain tumor had his doctor not told us, when he delivered the real diagnosis, that Graves' disease is often mistaken for something else. In fact, a century ago severe untreated Graves' disease could cause such alarming psychosis that it was sometimes misidentified as schizophrenia. I consoled myself with the thought that even the experts don't always get it right.

(It's wild how often chemical or physical abnormalities are attributed to mental illness or, even more oddly, supernatural bedevilment. Ancient Romans thought people who had seizures had a direct line of communication to the gods. Ancient Greeks thought they were possessed by demons. To be fair, who's to say it's wrong to think our skulls might be containers for brains but also for things beyond our understanding? Like the zigzagged lines on an EEG readout, things we can see often indicate things we cannot.)

John's doctor recommended a radiation procedure, then a daily pill forever after. Two decades later, John still takes his Synthroid every day. All that fear and confusion at first, but in the end, it was so simple.

When you're first diagnosed with a chronic health situation, figuring out how to treat it and live with it eats up a lot of time. Some conditions keep requiring that kind of attention, but some don't. Many you just get used to, and you don't even need to think about them most of the time. Epilepsy could be like that, we told our son, when he wondered, "Who should I tell?" Tell everyone who needs to know for safety reasons, we decided. Tell classmates, coaches, and teachers. Beyond that, we said, it's up to you. You might like for people to know, or you might hold off for a while. It's not like you need to announce it right off the bat every time you meet someone new. After all, it's not likely to come up in most situations, because your seizures will probably be well controlled with medication.

We didn't know that for sure, though. We only hoped it.

Medicine is chemistry and truth, but it is also art. It is data, but it's also interpretation of data, which is guessing. When MD told us that controlling seizures could be a process of trial and error, I hoped for a shorter trial and a little less error than in the case of my migraines. I hoped it would go more like when John got sick: diagnosis, treatment, end of problem. Although I knew it was scientifically impossible to pass down our own experiences to our son, to upload them into his cells, I kept thinking about our pasts as if they mattered to his present.

What I wanted for my son was a predictable, reliable treatment. We had just over two years until, if all went well, he would finish high school and leave home. Knowing that every medication change also came with months of adjusting to side effects, potentially medicating those side effects, and then adjusting to *those* medications, I felt like two years was barely enough time to get things sorted out.

The pill my son had begun taking—which was actually four enormous pills, taken at bedtime— was known to work extremely well at controlling seizures, but it also came with side effects. Thus far, he had only suffered one adverse reaction to the medicine, although it was a disappointing one: stomachaches that turned one of his great joys—eating—into a miserable trade-off. He could satisfy his hunger and dig into a burger or pizza, but within an hour he would suffer abdominal cramps so painful they made him double over. In theory, they would stop at some point when his body fully acclimated to the drug. No one knew when that would be.

Metabolizing the drug also put a strain on some patients' livers. To make sure the medicine didn't poison him instead of save him, he had to take an amino acid pill to boost his liver function and would have to go to the hospital to have a test tube full of blood drawn every six months to measure his liver enzymes. And because it was important not to stress the liver further, people taking this drug were strongly advised not to drink alcohol. At fifteen, he hadn't even started drinking, but still, he would have to make adjustments.

"So . . . in college . . . ?" he asked once, right after starting the medicine, when we were still reading up on its effects. This was my child who craved togetherness, being part of a group, having a team handshake. I knew he was picturing fraternity parties. I could give a lecture on how it's cool not to drink and he wasn't missing anything at all and there were plenty of nondrinkers out there on campuses across the country, or I could accept that he was processing what he saw as the loss of a rite of passage. I met him where he was.

"Well, there's always nonalcoholic beer." We talked about how perhaps he'd make friends by offering to be everyone's designated driver.

But that subject, too, was sensitive. Because no one knows whether they're on the right anti-seizure drug until it has proven itself by working well for a while, patients starting these drugs are advised not to drive. Our state ruled that a person had to be six months seizure-free before getting back on the road. Just two months away from the independence of earning his driver's license, my son had to stop practicing behind the wheel. For the next semester, he couldn't go anywhere unless a parent drove him or he hitched a ride with a friend. The countdown to freedom was set back half a year, and he knew that if he had another seizure it would reset.

For all our common understanding of "standard" milestones, it seems rare that anyone hits all of them in the exact same way on the same schedule. That becomes so obvious in adulthood—when we all break free of the school calendar and start to realize that we're each on our own path— but when you're a teenager, doing anything differently from what it looks like everyone else is doing makes you feel like a big, glaring exception.

I wished my son didn't have to feel that way. I wished he could rest easy, knowing the pills he swallowed would unfailingly protect him from another lightning strike. But no amount of hoping on my part, no volume of information I might hunt down and gather, not even having the greatest doctor and the strongest medicine—and the tremendous advantage of having access to both—would enable him to skip all this.

Everybody has something, and most things aren't so bad. All that's true, but there's more to it. You don't get to choose what your thing is, whether you get just one thing or more, or how your thing will respond to your efforts to manage it. And no matter how willingly you accept that about yourself, your compliance with fate doesn't earn you any say in anyone else's thing either. Not even your own child's.

No medication is 100 percent effective, MD told us. Figuring out the best one was part of the process.

"So we just wait," I said.

"We do the best we can to get it right the first time," MD said. "But yeah, then we wait."

DO YOU HEAR THE PEOPLE SING?

When it feels like you don't know how to save someone, you may try to save someone else—anyone else. Thus canine mealtime at our house became something much more than an attempt to get my dog to eat. At every breakfast and dinner with our short yellow mutt, Woodstock, I struck a silent deal. *If Woodstock eats today, it means my boy will be okay.*

For all the years of Woodstock's life, we had fretted. We had cajoled. We had added tasty tidbits to his food. We had examined his teeth. We had consulted our vet. We had tried various medicines and switched dog food brands. Nothing changed the fact that sometimes Woodstock ate and sometimes he did not. His periodic fasting lasted for anywhere from a day to a couple of days to off-and-on over a few weeks. We, his people, had never been able to decipher rhyme or reason behind it. We had never had a dog like this before, one who didn't eat. We were used to beagles, who danced on their hind legs to reach the bowl before we even set it down and hoovered up their kibbles, barely even chewing.

The rational side of my brain said to let it be. If he was hungry, he would eat. That's what we used to teach parents at the children's hospital. I wrote an educational brochure once, summarizing the lessons of a popular book at the time called *Child of Mine: Feeding with Love and Good Sense*. Written for parents of extremely picky eaters, it included a chapter called "Feeding Is Parenting" and put forth a theory that the parent and child each have a role at mealtime. A parent or caregiver's role is to prepare a selection of healthy food and put it on a plate; the child's role is to choose whether and how much to eat. There should never be bargaining, begging, or short-order-cookery in which the child yells, *"I want waffles!"* and the parent leaps from the table to fire up the griddle. If the kid feels hunger and wants to eat, they'll eat. If not, they won't, and the parent—who must not freak out about the child not eating—should calmly clear the plate at the end of mealtime. There may be ups and downs in the child's eating patterns, but they won't go hungry. This approach obviously didn't apply to children with serious eating disorders, but for many typically developing kids, it worked. Parents raved about how it changed their lives and made dinnertime more peaceful.

I didn't have children at the time, only a single dog who ate very well (our first beagle, Frances, may she rest). So I did not really grasp why this book had become a bestseller. *Must be a bummer for your kid not to eat,* I supposed. I also thought but did not say aloud, *Maybe those people need to stop getting so worked up about food. Just relax.* I had no experience with the panic that rises in a human heart when it's your job to take care of someone, but despite your efforts, they can't or won't respond to your care.

Later, I would understand. "How's he feeding?" the nurses would ask, popping their heads into my hospital room as I learned how to nurse my firstborn. At the time, I laughed at how the verb *feeding* made him sound like a piece of livestock. He was the piglet, and I was the trough. But I felt it, too, how primitively essential this function was, how little difference between animals and humans. We're all creatures. Everyone has to eat.

Feeding was so much of parenting, I would learn: Counting the ounce marks on the bottles that came with my breast pump. Whizzing up smoothies in the blender to make sure my preschoolers ate fruit. Watching a child pick the grains of rice out of a bowl of soup, leaving behind the chicken, the carrots, the broth. Saying I didn't believe in cooking separate "kid food," but then getting so tired of listening to children gag on sweet potatoes and spit their beans back onto their plates. Knowing that if I just gave them a pancake, they would eat and we could go have bath time and story time and all the other times that were easier. Giving them Popsicles when they were sick and refused water, because they have to stay hydrated, right?

Now, twenty years after I wrote those brochures about feeding, I was trying to feed Woodstock with love and good sense. Really, I was. Whenever I said, "Okay, have it your way," and took up his still-full bowl, he went about his day. He didn't beg later for the food he passed up. But within a few hours, his stomach would growl, a low rumble that grew through the day into an excruciating squeal so loud the person on the other end of a phone call once asked me, "What is that *sound?*" If Woodstock didn't eat for the rest of the day, he would begin vomiting frothy yellow acid around the house in discreet puddles, some of which I found immediately, others of which I stepped in days later. Clearly, his body needed food, whether his mind knew it or not.

How much easier everything would have been if I could have just asked, *What's going on? Did you hurt yourself? Are you sick?* and he could have answered.

I suspected Woodstock's feeding troubles went back to his origins as a pup. He and his siblings were born on the mean streets of Music City, found by a Good Samaritan, and taken into a rescue facility—I have no idea what happened to their mother, though I've often wondered—then immediately transferred to a veterinary clinic when they were discovered to have parvovirus. They required tube feeding and constant monitoring. Poor little Woodstock, separated from his mom and litter, fed through a tube. No wonder he didn't develop normal eating habits.

But he was our responsibility now, and that meant it was our job to make sure he ate. You can't adopt a pet and then go, *Oh well, this one's broken, what can you do?*

Except you can, unfortunately.

I can think of three frogs who would back me up on this, if they could.

The first: In college, I received a frog as a gift from a friend. He arrived along with a goldfish in a bowl of water with some pink rocks at the bottom. I named him Peeve and the fish Free Refills. My pets Peeve and Free Refills got along splendidly and spent many joyous months swimming and . . . swimming.

But unbeknownst to me, Peeve was plagued by dark compulsions. One afternoon I came back from class and found he had jumped out of his bowl. There he was, sizzling on the radiator like the lunch special on a hibachi. It was quite the grisly sight.

The second and third: About a decade ago, my children were given a pair of African dwarf water frogs as a present. (Now that I've mentioned gifted frogs twice, allow me to detour quickly to say that giving someone a pet without their prior approval isn't cool. No animal deserves to be the surprise new family member of a person who had no plans to care for it.) My kids were very young at the time, so let's be real—those frogs were my responsibility.

While Parcheesi torpedoed through the water like he was training for the Ironfrog, Snowflake flapped around in languid circles. At feeding time, Parcheesi gulped down his food pellets, but Snowflake only pretended to eat. Like Cookie Monster, he gummed his food—*mah mah mah*—but let it all fall out of his mouth, every time. Slowly, he wasted away until he looked like nothing more than an anatomical sketch of a frog on a scrap of wax paper, drifting through the water. One day we found his emaciated body tangled up in his tiny underwater bamboo tree, one leg wrapped around his own neck in a final act of acrobatic defiance. *Damn, Snowflake,* I thought. *That's intense.*

Two years passed. One morning, as we prepared to shake some frog food into the water, we discovered that Parcheesi had passed away in the night. We gave the tank a jiggle to be sure. He did not move. So I scooped up his rigid corpse with a spoon, laid it on a paper towel, and gathered the family. We all said some somber words and reflected on Parcheesi's time with us.

Just before we took him outside to bury him under the same maple tree where we had laid Snowflake to rest, the kids decided to throw a few food pellets into the shroud that held his body, since he always liked those so much.

And that's when he woke up.

Everyone screamed.

He did this on two more occasions before he finally died for good.

What I left out of those three tales is how I stood over the frogs' tanks, watching them. How I researched frog illnesses and consulted other frog owners and tried to figure out what went wrong.

To the children I said, "These things happen," and to John I joked about being a frog killer, because what else could I do? I tried to take care of them, and I failed, and they died. If I couldn't create a buffer between my heart and every loss, how would I live in this world? How would I get behind the wheel of a car every day and drive while looking out a windshield speckled with the sticky confetti of tiny legs and translucent wings? Where is the fill line that indicates my maximum capacity for grief? Before insects, fine. But before or after dime-size frogs I didn't ask to have?

All of this is why I will never have another frog. And it all came back to me when Woodstock started his hunger strikes.

I would not accept that Woodstock would starve.

None of us would. John tried moving Wood-stock's food from his bowl to a plate. My son tried hand-feeding him, lying down at Wood-stock's level on the floor, patiently holding out a few kibbles in his palm, speaking softly, sweetly, "Look, man, it's good. Yum." But Woodstock turned his head this way and that, like a kid clamping their lips shut when you do "here comes the choo-choo" at their face with a spoonful of squash.

It is the greatest blessing of a dog owner's life to find a dog sitter who genuinely cares for your dogs, and we hit the lottery when we found two. Steph and Nathan, a young couple, never balked at the prospect of caring for a dog who might or might not eat on a given day. Perhaps his eating situation seemed like nothing compared to the pantry-raiding, shoe-destroying, dawn-waking whims of our beagle, Eleanor Roosevelt, whom they also tolerated beyond all reason. They did the job diligently and lovingly—trying to get Woodstock to eat twice a day, never worrying too much when he skipped a few meals, and texting us updates when we were away, so we knew how he was doing.

One summer while we were visiting family, we got a message from Nathan, saying that he'd been spinning the latest Kanye West tunes on a speaker in the kitchen while making the dogs' breakfast and that the music seemed to act as an appetite enhancer. He didn't want to say anything at first, in case it was a fluke, but for four days so far Woodstock was eating full meals to the album *Ye*. All we had to do when we got home was put on his new favorite music and Woodstock would eat.

So once we returned, we played Kanye twice a day, and for weeks and weeks Woodstock ate. His hair grew shinier, his sprints around the backyard more energetic. As I watched over his meals, I often found myself listening—"Shit could get menacin', frightenin' "—and asking Woodstock, "Is that how you feel, buddy?"

A few months later, John and I both had to pull a week of long workdays, so we put our daughter in charge of the daily dog-feeding routine. When I checked in on Wednesday to see how things were going, she reported that she'd switched Woodstock from Kanye to Broadway.

I shouldn't have been surprised. My theater-loving child subscribes to *Playbill* magazine, gets news alerts from Broadway.com, and can tell you exactly who's playing which role in every musical currently running in both New York and London. But I was flabbergasted. Why hadn't it occurred to me to change the music? I'd blindly accepted Kanye as the cure when maybe any song would do.

That weekend, I cued up "Rocket Man" by

Elton John and put Woodstock's bowl of food on the floor. No dice.

I tried Prince. Nope. Fleetwood Mac? No. What about going back to Kanye? That didn't work anymore either.

My daughter had managed to transfer Woodstock's loyalties entirely to the original Broadway cast recording of *Les Misérables*.

There was no fighting it; it worked. So early one morning, as Woodstock lay on the floor before his bowl and the actors bellowed, "Do you hear the people sing?" I sang to my dog, "Do you hear the people? I do! I hear them sing! The singing makes me hungry. Are you hungry? Mmmmmm, singing!"

He sniffed his food.

I sang, "Do you hear the people sing? Singing the songs of hungry dogs . . ."

Is there any musical one can listen to twice a day, every day, without going mad?

Woodstock lay there, drooling, deciding whether he was ready to take that first bite. This was part of the routine, always. There were moments as I waited for him to eat when I was so tired, I folded my arms upon the counter and rested my forehead on them. Maybe I was tired because Eleanor Roosevelt had awakened me at 5 a.m. to ask a question she could only ask in a loud howl and that no one could answer. Maybe I was tired because I was sitting at the kitchen counter in the dark of morning, researching amino acid supplements on my laptop, hoping to find the one that would best help my son's liver metabolize his medicine.

Maybe I was placing my head upon my crossed arms because Jean Valjean was singing a prayer, asking God to protect the young revolutionary Marius:

Bring him peace, bring him joy
He is young, he is only a boy
You can take, you can give
Let him be, let him live

He is only a boy. Let him live.

Just as I was starting to hallucinate that I was a Parisian street urchin, Woodstock stood and took a tentative step toward his bowl. "Will you join in our crusade?" the chorus called, and he took one little brown rock of dog food between his teeth and held it there for a few seconds before biting down. He was joining the crusade! He crunched, swallowed, waited a few seconds, then took another. I could not scratch my nose or adjust my position in my chair or walk over to the coffeemaker, because if I did, he would stop and lie down and would not be convinced to try again for at least a day.

It was strange and ridiculous, and I'm glad no one saw me there holding my breath and waiting for a dog to eat, but I did it. Of course I did it. I was tired, and I was desperate, and I needed to know I could successfully look after the living beings in my care.

No one ever said our ministrations to the ones we love have to be dignified, anyway. At least this one was easy. All I had to do was be still and let the music play.

PART TWO

CALM YOURSELF

I started meditating when my sleep began diminishing. My brain has always served up an overflowing junk box of worries and trivia to sort as soon as I lie down and resume sorting immediately upon waking up. This has never been a fun way to start and end bedtime, but at least in the middle I could fall asleep and dream—usually about living in a house made of marshmallow furniture that I can eat because it constantly regenerates fresh marshmallow upholstery. Over time, though, the worries began advancing at the borders, keeping me up later and waking me earlier. I was greeting each day feeling unrefreshed and under siege.

I wasn't sure I could start meditating on my own, given that, at least as I understood it, meditation required quieting your thoughts, which was the very thing I needed help to do. So to shush the fretful voice in my head, I decided to replace it with some peaceful guided meditations I found online. I downloaded a sample:

Begin by finding a comfortable position, the narrator said, every word a swelling, floating soap bubble—a full sigh in between each. She sounded like she had just been shot in the flank with one of those darts they use on animals that escape the zoo, and that seemed like the right level of tranquilization for me.

It has been a couple of years now, and I still listen to guided meditations in the mornings. Not every day, but most days. People ask, "Does it work?" I guess that depends on your definition of success. Have I managed to achieve total stillness? Have I stopped time, for even a few minutes? Am I slowing the speed at which life hurtles toward its mysterious black hole of an ending? Has my mind stopped churning? No, no, no, and oh hell no.

But I can confirm that now, when I stir at 3 a.m., I often go back to sleep, because I know the meditation is coming up in a few hours and I look forward to it as if it's an appointment with my own brain. I'm not sure at all that this is what it was supposed to do, but it lets me consolidate my night thinking into one dawn session, and that's helpful.

I turn on the recording right after I turn off my alarm, as soon as I'm aware of being awake but before I'm all the way there. Still in the liminal space between sleep-world and real-world, I lie with my eyes closed, right where I slept, in a bed that is maybe or maybe not made of marshmallow. It goes more or less like so:

Let your limbs rest comfortably.

How many vertebrae does a human spine have?

Breathe in. Breathe out. Let the breath relax the tension in your arms and hands, legs and feet.

Sometimes, when the backs of my knees itch, I feel scratchy tights I'm not wearing and hear organ music.

Now bring your focus inward.

Remember that movie *Howard the Duck*?

Today, you're going to practice being present.

Remember that time I was looking for my planner and then I realized I'd lost it in an airport the day before? And instead of screaming or tearing up the house, I just sat still at my kitchen table and quietly, mentally bled out? I was very present in that moment.

You're going to let go of what doesn't concern you.

Remember when I had a cake from a fancy bakery sent to a friend, but something went wrong in the shipping and it showed up on her doorstep half-squashed, the icing all runny? I would never have known the cake was ruined when it arrived, except that she called and said, "Wow, I just got a box of melted cake. You should see it. There's a chocolate river on my porch."

I'm never using that bakery again.

But also: Why did she tell me that? Wouldn't it have been nicer to say, "Wow, thank you for sending me a cake," and keep the rest to herself? That's what I would have done.

You're going to release yourself from fixating on the thoughts and actions of others.

I think sometimes I want people to be better than they are, so I treat them as if they're as good as I wish they were, and then somehow I'm surprised when they behave like the person they really are, not the person I pretend they are.

You are even going to release yourself from fixating on your own thoughts.

Take my neighbor, for instance, who put a giant banner in his front yard for the terrible candidate running for office. I'm not talking "terrible" like their tax plan isn't my favorite. I'm talking *terrible,* as in, given their blatant disregard for and possibly even hatred of fellow humans, not to mention the rest of the earth, you have to consider whether this candidate is on some kind of slow-motion suicide mission, hell-bent on taking us all along for the ride.

Rather than trying to catch them and hold them, let your thoughts flow past you, as you remain rooted to the earth.

Also, this candidate has crude manners and a whiny voice, and just the sight of that pompous face makes me think morbid thoughts. I don't really believe anyone should intentionally hurt anyone else—no one should meet any end other than their natural one in due time—but can't I have just a tiny fantasy? For example, what if NASA could convince this candidate that they're the only person smart and handsome and brave enough for an elite mission to lay claim to the outer reaches of space. They could say, "We want you to *own* the galaxy! Everyone knows you're the one to do it!" And then we could launch the shuttle out there with an extra-large tank of fuel and just, you know, see how it goes.

Rather than try to catch the thoughts as they come and go, you will accept that movement is constant. We are surrounded by change.

I could put a letter in my neighbor's mailbox. Not a scathing one or anything. A kind one. I could be a bridge builder and appeal to all the things I know we have in common, like . . . mailboxes. "I can see that you, too, have small gravel along the side of your driveway," I might write, "and this makes me understand that in our hearts, we are not all that different."

Or I could sneak over every morning, while it's still dark, and add some text to the banner. Just a little something.

If your mind has drifted, return your focus to the breath. Keep your attention on the inhale and the exhale.

I would need one of those jumbo Sharpies.

If you notice you're still having thoughts, acknowledge them and release them without judgment. Say, "Thinking, thinking, thinking."

Thinking, thinking, thinking.

Remember, you can allow contradictions to exist without trying to solve them.

Contradictions. Yes. I can handle those. Like that time Woodstock ran to the back door with something to show me, dropping his gift at my feet, wagging his tail and tap-dancing with joy, and then I picked it up, and it was a rabbit's leg—a perfect, silky-furred foot, its delicate metatarsal bones cleanly broken off at the joint—and I said, "Oh God, oh no, oh Jesus," and also, "So nice, thank you, good boy."

If you get distracted by a sensation in your body, like back pain or tightness in your chest, say, "Feeling, feeling, feeling."

Feeling, feeling, feeling.

Remember that movie about the lawyer who fought DuPont on behalf of the town in West Virginia that had chemicals dumped into its drinking water? And how it turns out that the chemical waste of factories that produce things we use all the time, like plastic and gasoline and cookware, is everywhere now? It's in the blood of humans and bears and fish all over the world. Bodies can't break these chemicals down, because they were created to be indestructible, so the chemicals are breaking us down instead, causing tumors and endocrine disorders and reproductive problems. There is no way on earth to get that garbage out of our blood. We're just walking around with it. And we're still using the things the companies made with these chemicals, because we can't seem to stop. We're too far gone.

I wonder how the people who run those companies sleep at night. I wonder if they can remember the last good day they lived before they became someone who would trade life on earth for the business of selling laundry detergent and nonstick pans. I wonder if they go around thinking, *God, I* love *plastic spatulas. I'd do anything for them!*

Feeling, feeling, feeling.

Let your thoughts drift past,

I wonder if anyone in the world feels like they're doing a good job, even the people who really are doing good. I wonder . . .

as if on a breeze.

. . . if whoever wrote the song about Rudolph the Red-Nosed Reindeer thought about adding a verse where Rudolph wrestles with imposter syndrome.

As you let the breeze blow by, keep your focus on your breath.

If I wrote it, I might add some lines about how Rudolph wonders whether Santa only hired him because Donner is his dad. About how Rudolph stays up thinking that when the novelty of his glowing nose wears off, the whole North Pole is going to realize he's a fraud. A fluke. And then what? He'll have to go join Blinky and Sparkle wearing ornaments on their antlers and eating Quaker Oats out of a bucket at the Tampa Holiday Wonderland, that's what.

And now, as we wind down, bring your attention back to the room.

I didn't mean to think about reindeer.
I always mean to let my thoughts drift on the breeze.

Check in with your body.

Remember when I took video tap-dancing lessons, but I only took the same beginner lesson three times and then I never learned any more steps or even ordered tap shoes?
I wonder if I would have taken that first lesson if I'd known I wasn't ever going to get past it.

Wiggle your fingers and toes.

People say that all the time: "It wasn't supposed to end like this." They really mean, "I didn't *want* it to end like this." Nobody's a fortune-teller. You can't say the ending is a betrayal of the beginning—because in the beginning you couldn't possibly have known what the ending would be. You only know the ending you guessed. The one you assumed.

If you look at an ending you don't like as if it has forsaken its beginning, it'll make you resent beginnings. You'll call the beginnings mistakes. You'll say, "I never should have . . ." and you'll always be full of regret.

No one knows how anything is going to turn out, which means you can't get all indignant because it turned out differently. There is no *differently*. There's only the way it turns out. There's only the ending that was always going to happen; you just didn't know it.

Unless: All the molecules of the world are shimmering on standby, ready to turn into any number of endings, right up until the moment one sticks. And everything we do, in every minute, every second, rearranges the molecules until the music stops, like musical chairs.

Have a wonderful day.

I'm trying.

SERIOUSLY

At a professional reception a few years ago, a person with whom I had enough in common to be at the same events but whom I didn't really know looked my outfit up and down and said, "Well, aren't you cute?"

I had on a tasteful black sweater with opaque black tights, black flats, and a short, multicolored skirt sewn out of a fabulous and entirely man-made fabric that didn't even try to authentically imitate either feathers or fur but rather seemed some fuzzy combination of both. I cannot over-state the skirt's coziness or my fondness for it. It made me feel like a forest animal in formal wear, and it always perked me up, even if I was tired and in no mood to socialize.

"Thanks!" I said with a smile, tipping my clear plastic cup of lukewarm Chardonnay in greeting.

My fellow partygoer continued, "Of course, no one will ever take you seriously if you keep dressing that way," and walked off into the crowd.

I stopped smiling.

Okay, first of all, imagine being the kind of person who can't help saying something like that.

Second, imagine believing there is nothing more important than being taken seriously.

Third, imagine being unable to take someone seriously because of their outfit. What would that mean? That you have exactly one track in your mind and it can hold either respectful, intellectual thoughts or a fun skirt, but not both? How easily disrupted you'd be. What if you'd been working all your life on some scientific pursuit—a theory that proves the existence of extraterrestrial life, say—and then you met a researcher who had discovered the elusive piece of information that would fill in the last stubborn gap in your theory, but the researcher was wearing a rainbow-sequined jacket? Would witnessing their magnificent outfit render you unable to consider their data, causing you to abandon your lifelong goal? Come on now.

I wish I'd called after this person as they walked away, "How about my resumé? Would you take that seriously? My diploma? The books I've written? What if the skirt were longer, would that help? What if I made a deep-thinking face *like this? Growwwwl.*"

Consider the qualities that are often assumed to be in opposition to one another. Excellence and humility. Intelligence and humor. A fake-fur skirt at a work party. My fondness for contrast isn't unique to women or to Southerners, but I do think many Southern women learned it from our mamas. Do your work, earn that degree, get that promotion, and *also* perfect your recipe for pimiento cheese. Curl your hair before you methodically destroy opposing counsel in court. Develop a world-famous economic theory and also have a signature dance move that brings the house down. Spend some effort to express sweetness or festivity or silliness, even when—especially when—there are important matters to attend to. Taking things seriously without taking yourself too seriously keeps people on their toes, not to mention makes life more interesting.

I like how spontaneous goodwill can spread from person to person like champagne spilling over a tower of coupe glasses. I smile at someone, they feel like smiling, and they smile at the next person they pass. You say hello and compliment my shoes, I light up, and I offer a friendly word to somebody else. I tell someone excitedly about something good—a baby panda was born! There's a great new movie out! Two letters are burned out on that neon sign over there and now it spells something obscene!—and then they, too, look around, notice something delightful, and share it.

But every now and then the chain breaks, and I encounter someone so put off by genuine enthusiasm that they feel compelled to attack it. I never know quite how to respond.

I spoke at a fundraising event several years ago, and toward the end I took a minute to thank not only the attendees for showing up but also the host for having us and the donors for footing the bill. Saying thank you seemed the right thing to do, and I meant it. Afterward a woman approached me at the foot of the stage, scowling, and said, "You say 'thank you' too much."

I struggled to answer her. Instinctively, I began to thank her for sharing her opinion, "Oh, well, thank you for coming. I mean, um . . . thanks for . . . well . . . just . . . okay . . . have a good day," which probably only made her madder. She hitched her purse over her shoulder and turned around as I continued bumbling.

I wish I'd had a snappy comeback ready before she walked away. Moments later, I thought, *Oh honey, when it comes to saying thank you, there is* no such thing *as too much.*

Doesn't it get exhausting? All that resistance to joy, all that energy spent trying to darken other people's light?

Don't smile too much. Don't say thank you too much. Don't put your hair in too high of a ponytail. Don't wear bright colors. Don't wear any colors. Don't wear that neckline. No, not that one either. Don't wear lipstick. Are you sure those earrings are for daytime? Be serious. Be so serious you're dull. Be so serious you're rude. Be so serious you're miserable.

No, thank you.

Here's another one: "She seems so . . . happy." I heard a woman I'd just met say this about another woman at a conference, in the same tone of voice one might say, "It looks . . . infected." We were standing around the gray-carpeted hotel hospitality room, picking at snacks on the refreshment table. She was talking about the person she was about to go onstage with, who was across the room. She had never met this person in real life but had sized her up based on various interviews and social media posts. Another person in our group nodded and grimaced. "Yeah, kind of a cheerleader, right?"

It bothered me then and it bothers me still. How would her happiness have prevented a great co-presenting experience? I supposed if the subject of the presentation had been "Sadness: The Only Real Emotion," a perky demeanor would have been off-brand. But otherwise, what's so wrong with projecting a sense of good cheer?

I was never a cheerleader, except for exactly two weeks in ninth grade, when the tiny, nerdy school I went to decided that even though they didn't have enough guys to field a football team, they could have cheerleaders for soccer games. After the first few team meetings, it was decided that the scrawniest members of the team would be the ones who had to learn how to fly up in the air and be caught by their classmates. Everyone looked at me then, and I said, "Fuck this, thank you, but I'm going back to Latin Club."

So no, I have no experience as a real cheerleader. But I try to cheer for all sorts of things: books, art, animals, underdogs, people trying to figure themselves out, people toiling away at unglamorous work purely because they care and want to make a difference. (Go, scientists!) Few things cheer me up as much as giving a pep talk that cheers up someone else. Why wouldn't we want to do that for one another as much as we can?

John does a funny thing in traffic. If someone cuts him off or veers in and out of his lane and he ends up next to them at a stoplight, he cranes his neck sideways and glares at them. It's as if he's scolding them with his facial expression, like they'll sense his eyes on them and think, *Why is that man looking at me? Oh, it must have been the way I was tailing his car back there. What a mistake I've made! The regrets! How will I live with myself?* In reality, the other driver never notices. John is wasting his energy, wanting some kind of revenge he's not going to get. It's one of my favorites of his habits, because it's so hilariously out of step with the rest of his personality. Here he is, one of the most calm and bighearted people I know, giving people this small, spiteful stare, because he wants them to feel bad about their behavior. It makes me laugh.

I love that he does such a human thing, because I am human, too. I understand the desire to hurt someone after I've been hurt, to make someone else experience disappointment to match my own. I understand the impulse to pick a fight with a circumstantial nemesis, a person who's not really my enemy—not in any way that truly matters—but whom I've cast in the moment as a contextual adversary. It allows me to release the pressure valve on any real, meaningful anger I may be experiencing while also indulging the urge to kick up a tussle. I find, when it feels like everything in the world is out of my control, it's better not to take that madness out on my own family and friends. That's what grudges are for.

For example, I confess: One of the things that keeps me going is a hot little engine inside my soul, chugging away until the next time I run into the person who insulted my skirt, whom I haven't seen since that night. I hope it's at another professional party, and I hope I have the better seat. In fact, I fantasize that we'll see each other again at an award ceremony in which I'm being honored with something amazing and ridiculous, like a newly invented Pulitzer Prize for Patient Manners While Standing in Line. I hope they hear the speech someone gives about me and go, "Wait, isn't that the woman whose skirt I couldn't take seriously?" And if we run into each other at the bar afterward, I could fix this person with an evil-eyed stare, and maybe just as I'm about to lean close and whisper something that would metaphorically remove their kneecaps, they'll announce, "I underestimated you, and I was wrong!"

It's an entertaining train of thought. I just don't want to let that kind of thinking get out of control.

Creative types are always talking about "world building." When a screenwriter or novelist tells a story, they have to both create and adhere to the rules of the world in which their story takes place. I think we do that in our minds as well. We create worlds. As soon as you decide to project your misery onto someone else, you start building a grudge world. Every time you visit it, you lay another brick. I think some people build grudges up in such detail that their grudge worlds become too big and too real. They stop living in the actual world and begin living full-time in a universe built by resentment and anger. The grudge turns into something dark and obsessive. And when a person confuses a grudge with a real problem, they may start making real-world decisions using grudge-world logic. They think they really hate people they don't even know.

I don't want to do that. I play around sometimes in these made-up worlds, in which I cast myself as a hero and a snippy person at a party as a villain. The conflict I imagine between us stands in for how mad I am about so many things I can't do anything about. But I think I would prefer to live here, in reality.

If it's true that the skirt insulters and thank-you refusers of the world are unhappy themselves, if they act out because it seems unfair for everyone else to be chipper while they feel so glum, I wish I could make them understand that there's no need to tear everyone else down. No one else is completely happy either. I don't wear cute skirts and say thank you because I'm free from fury and despair. I'm not smiling at people as a way of denying the existence of failure, frustration, loneliness, or loss.

Sometimes I don't know how any of us go on. Sometimes I fear there's no way our species will survive our own self-destructive choices. Sometimes I feel so gut punched by the backward deal of the universe—that if you're really lucky, you get people in your life to love, and then, over time, they will all either leave you or die—that I am angry at *life*. Actually, not sometimes. Always. I always feel that way. I don't always actively think about it, but it's in there.

At the same time, I am always looking for

some gratitude, warmth, or hope. I often have to really search for it, but when I see something that makes me feel joy—even just a tiny odd hardly anything—you're damn right I applaud it. Way to go, adorable cat on a leash! Thank you, server who brought my hot pizza! Kudos, writers of a TV show that made me laugh! Hallelujah, sunshine after a week of storms! Yay for a good hair day, yippee for hot coffee, huzzah for an outfit that puts bounce in my step.

If I can scrape up some evidence of a thing made beautifully or a gesture made kindly, then I can believe, for a few seconds, that this world *is* careful and kind. And if I can believe that, I can believe it is safe to let the people I love walk around out there. It's my own attempt at foresparkling, seeking out hints of good, even planting them myself, so I can believe there's more good to come. It might all be superstition, just mental magic, but why not try?

So I say *yes* for things that offer some pleasure. *Yes* for people who choose to be friendly. *Yes* for any glimmer of light through all the darkness. I mean that *yes*. I need it. Seriously.

TO THE WOMAN
SCREAMING ON THE QUAD

I heard about her embarrassing episode after the fact, from a college admissions officer who gleefully regaled a crowd with it and turned it into a cautionary tale. It was just after the end of my son's sophomore year in high school, six months after his seizure, and we were taking advantage of a family road trip to stop along the way and do the incredible, inevitable thing—our first college tour. As a few assembled families gathered for an information session before the walking portion, our guide shared some words of advice for parents. The main lesson: that during our children's college search process we must resist our natural urge to transform into overbearing monsters.

Everyone had seen the stories on the news about the celebrity parents who paid a "consultant" to bribe coaches and falsify admissions files in order to gain their children's acceptance to elite universities. I understood why the warnings were necessary. Parents sometimes imposed their own desires on their kids' college searches for all sorts of reasons. (Was I acting on my own behalf more than his when, a few months after this, I took my son to tour my alma mater? Yes, I confess:

I thought I might sidestep the whole "leaving home" thing if he enrolled somewhere that felt like home to me. He wasn't interested.)

Still, I bristled at the way this admissions officer implied that without some strong redirection every parent was a meddling shrew, especially mothers.

"I'll give you an example," he said before the tour. "Last fall, a mom and her daughter came in, and it was obvious the visit was the mother's idea. The mom asked all the questions, and the girl just stared at her shoes. She couldn't even muster the enthusiasm for a decent handshake! And then, somehow, they got separated from the rest of the tour. When our tour guide walked back to find them," and here he lowered his voice to a conspiratorial stage whisper, "the woman was standing in the middle of the quad having a *screaming match* with her daughter."

The crowd reacted to his story about the mother from hell with a cascade of gasps and laughs. Someone behind me blurted, "Oh my God, *can you imagine?*"

I didn't laugh. I could imagine.

Oh, screaming-on-the-quad lady. I'm sorry about your day.

I don't know who you are or where you are now. Maybe you deserve every bit of ridicule and judgment that admissions officer dishes out when he performs your story for a captive audience. Maybe you're a grown-up brat raising a teenage brat and you scream on every quad you visit, not to mention in restaurants, on sidewalks, and at home. Maybe all you do is scream, scream, scream.

Or maybe you had to take three days off work to go on that college tour.

I'm just imagining here, but perhaps: You filed your vacation paperwork so you could take this trip with your kid, even though it's the busiest season in your job at, I don't know, let's say an insurance company, where it's your responsibility to train new hires. You had to train someone else to train the newbies just so you could leave town, and you had to beg your sociopathic boss for the time off, even though she's legally required to grant you the vacation days in your employment contract. But you knew it was worth it.

You like your job, although your coworkers drive you nuts sometimes and you feel horrible about how much time you've been spending at work lately. Your daughter has been, to use the 1980s term you never had to use because your mother was always there when you got home from school, a "latchkey kid" for the past year. She lets herself into a quiet house when she gets off the bus; digs in the pantry for a packaged snack of some sort because when on earth would you have had time to make dried-fruit bars or whole-grain cookies? She feeds the cat and does homework alone until you get home. You wanted these three days to be about being present, looking each other in the eyes, having long talks in the car while driving from college town to college town. You wanted this to be an episode of *Gilmore Girls*. You wanted to make up for everything you've done wrong as a mother while you were trying to do everything right.

Five campuses in three days are a lot, but you figured if you crammed them into one trip, you wouldn't have to ask for time off work again. Your daughter picked all five schools for their strong art history programs. That's what she's into, she says, after taking an art history class first semester junior year. You are excited that she is willing to tell you something she's excited about, because for the past year she has told you less and less about what she's thinking.

This is developmentally appropriate—children are supposed to grow away from their parents. But she used to tell you everything, and you miss her so much. Sometimes you can tell she misses you a bit, too. "I love you, Mama," she said the other night before she went to bed. At her core, she's the same sweet girl she has always been— the joy of your life, who used to creep into your room at night and sleep curled up against your side, under your armpit. As a gangly preteen, she tentatively asked you to help her pick out mascara at the drugstore, and you thought, *See, we have a bond other mothers and daughters don't have; she's letting me in.* But now all of a sudden, she has taken to snapping, "What?" when you speak to her. In public, you must not use any pet names or make any references to private jokes, because she will roll her eyes and turn away from you.

You know she'll be back. The parenting articles say this behavior is normal. You can see her true self, that radiant soul, through all the rebellious posturing. She cried the other day when her best friend's dog died, but when you leaned in to hug her she angled her elbows up like a protective gate to block you out, and that hurt like a slap.

This morning, the last day of your trip, you woke up in side-by-side double beds to the parched blast of the hotel air unit and the sound of your phone chiming 7 a.m. She was in no mood to be nudged into the shower and down to the hotel lobby for a rubbery bagel and a paper cup of reconstituted orange juice, but you couldn't be late. By the time you arrived at the historic house that serves as the university's admissions office, she had said exactly one full sentence all morning: "Whatever continent that 'continental breakfast' came from, it's a sad continent."

You paused on the porch and said, "Smile, please." Your daughter stretched her lips around her clenched teeth. The face she was making would have been humorous if she hadn't been making it to show how hell-bent she was on being mean. It's almost exhausting—almost irritating even to her, it seems—what a compulsion her new meanness is. She *must* hurt you. She *must* insult you. She *must* make sure you know that you disgust her. She is possessed by the need to wound you. You knew this difficult stage of growing up was coming, but you thought it would be funny, a farcical phase you'd both laugh about. "Oh, adolescence!"

"I'm not asking much," you said before both of you walked through the door. "Just try to look like you're glad to be here. Or at least not angry to be here. These people have never met you before."

When the tour guide set off with the group, your daughter walked slowly, falling to the back of the pack. "Hustle now," you said. "Get up there where you can hear." She slowed more. Your phone sounded a Caribbean drumbeat from your purse, alerting you to yet more new texts this morning from work, none of them urgent. None of them had been urgent for the past two days; still, they had been buzzing your phone day and night just to make sure you were aware that they were aware that you weren't there. Your daughter glared at you as you slid your hand into your purse to silence the phone.

A few minutes later, you touched her shoulder as the tour rounded a corner approaching the

Humanities building, "Can you think of a question?"

She did not acknowledge your prompt. The kids are supposed to talk on these tours. Asking questions is a way to show "demonstrated interest," which is a big deal. Every interaction is watched, remembered, recorded. The tour guide would give a report to her superiors later, in which she would name the students who spoke and the ones who didn't.

A fortuitous opening occurred when the guide stopped to let the group file past her into the dining hall. As the other parents and children stepped forward to peer around at the vaulted ceiling and long tables, you and your daughter found yourselves standing right next to the guide, who asked, "So what other schools are you looking at?"

"Mmm, not sure," your daughter said.

Not sure? What were those four tours you just took? Your daughter seemed to be putting all the effort she had into putting no effort into anything, arranging her face into an expression of exaggerated boredom.

As the other families left the dining hall and the group proceeded along the path toward the dorms, you reached out and took hold of your daughter's wrist.

"I have asked you three times, nicely, to participate in this tour. I know you're tired.

I'm tired. All you have to do is engage, please. In twenty minutes we're done. How hard is this?"

"I am engaging," she said, gritting her teeth.

"You're *not*."

The last stragglers of the tour group disappeared into the hulking brick dorm. The heavy black door closed behind them. Your purse vibrated against your ribs as your daughter yanked her arm away.

"Well, now I don't even know where they're going, so maybe if you want me to do the tour so much, you shouldn't keep making us stop."

"Why are you fighting me? This whole trip is for you. All you have to do is pay attention for a little while."

You wanted her to have options. You wanted everyone who met her to see what you see, which is that she is a kind person. She is a curious person. But she was not being kind that day. She was not being curious. She was throwing away her moment to show her real self to these people, after you did everything to get her here.

"I can't pay attention if you keep telling me to ask questions every five minutes!"

"I'll stop telling you to ask questions when you start showing the tiniest *fucking bit of interest and gratitude*."

And just then, the tour guide was somehow standing two feet away.

126

"Did you . . . want to see the dorms?" she asked.

She'd heard everything. Or at least enough.

It's a common saying—"when someone shows you who they are, believe them." I know there's truth in it. Still, it makes me cringe sometimes, because what if you get only a moment with someone and what they show you is a moment of weakness, a glimpse at some elemental human ugliness that they normally suppress? What if what you saw and what they meant were not the same? What if you've seen a good person in a bad moment, or simply a human person in a transitional moment, when they are exhausted by the work of becoming who they will be?

We all exist to one another as snippets of witnessed behavior. Everything we've ever done, no matter how true or false to our nature, makes us the kind of person who does that thing—at least to anyone who was there for it.

It's not that these glimpses aren't our real selves. Maybe they are. Maybe that's all real selfhood is: a pileup of moments. God forbid we be locked for all eternity into a replay of our lowest moments, though. What a great gift it would be to grant one another the grace of accepting who we've turned into, the self we fought to be.

I empathized with the mother who screamed on

the quad, because although she wasn't me, she could have been. After all, I was beginning the process of saying goodbye to my children, and it was hard. I didn't know what I was doing. What if she didn't either? Even when I am doing the best I can, I still come awfully close to yelling *fuck* in public every now and then, and I'd just as soon a man with a microphone not turn it into a story about the nature of mothers. Sometimes we just have to scream.

This kind of empathy can be useful. For example, when I hear a siren, I remember the morning in the ambulance. That memory makes me better, kinder.

This is what I mean: If I'm in traffic and I see a car refusing to pull over to make way for an emergency vehicle, remembering helps me to believe that the driver of the car is not evil, just blissfully ignorant. They're not proof that humanity has gone down the drain, that we've given up on one another, that we don't even care enough to save one another's lives. Anyone who has ever called an ambulance would pull over so fast they'd have one tire in a ditch. So they must never have made such a call. They must never have watched their own fingers pushing the buttons "9-1-1," never said, "Hurry, hurry, please hurry."

Maybe that's their problem, something that has

probably been my problem more times than I have ever known—too much good luck.

Or maybe it isn't. Maybe the driver who refuses to give up their spot in the turn lane for an ambulance is a total slime bag. I don't get to know. So I tell myself how awful it is that they don't know better and how wonderful it is that they have made it this long without knowing.

Otherwise, when an ambulance speeds past and I look ahead and see it stuck behind an SUV idling brazenly at an intersection, I can't help but hate the driver of the SUV. What if a building has collapsed or a train has derailed? What if a child has lost consciousness and time is running out? I'm already pulled over as far to the side of the road as I can be, worried for whomever that ambulance is headed to pick up. It doesn't do anyone any good for me to be worried and also full of hate. As much as I might have wished it as a child, my feelings can't move objects. So when the rage blazes through me, I force myself to remember my own ride alongside my son in an ambulance and give the SUV driver the benefit of the doubt. I need to believe that they will understand one day. They will regret the long seconds they sat there flashing their blinker. When that time comes and they've made the call, I hope every car in their path pulls over.

I have to try to love that driver the way I try to love that screaming woman on the quad. It's a glass-half-empty, glass-half-full kind of thing: Better to believe the world is at least half-full of decent intentions than to focus on how it's also half-full of assholes.

Woman on the quad, if you're real and if you're out there: I think of you often. I don't know what kind of person you are. All I know about you is that you screamed at your kid in public one time. And now, to the other people in that instant with you, you are forever a woman who screams at her kid in public. For all I know, you're as terrible as that admissions guy made you out to be, but I hope you're not. I hope the rest of your life doesn't feel like that afternoon did. I hope you don't even see this—and that you never find out they tell this story about you.

THE SIX STAGES OF FINDING OUT YOU HAVE HIGH CHOLESTEROL

If our bodies had any respect for us, they'd stagger their breakdowns—not just within a single individual, but within a family. Both parents in one household would never get a stomach virus at the same time, for instance, leaving a baby effectively parentless but for the two shivering, moaning people-husks on the bathroom floor. Calamities would spread themselves out a bit.

A cholesterol problem would not show up to complicate the life of a human being who already carries stress in her back—isn't one overreactive body part enough?—and can barely make time to go to physical therapy, much less to a lab to get blood drawn. Something so mundane would not demand attention while a person is trying to focus her attention on everyone else, including a child she must drive to his own suddenly numerous doctor's appointments. A bunch of cells would not throw a tantrum in her veins just as she is trying to focus on her top priority: keeping the rest of her family alive.

But they would, actually, because chemistry doesn't care about anyone's life. And when that happens, when some molecules turn on other molecules and cause trouble you can't ignore, it unfolds in predictable stages.

1. Denial. This phase actually comes before the test results, even before the test. These are the years in which the body quietly ages while the mind neglects to acknowledge the passage of time. Camped out mentally at some age in the past, you turn thirty-five, forty, forty-five . . .

In my denial phase, I might have noticed that while some clothes that fit a decade ago still fit, some did not anymore, but I also thought, *Well, styles have changed, and maybe I wore that sweater too tight back then.* The zippers on my boots went only halfway up before stopping, and I thought, *When did my calves solidify like this?* But overall, I looked fine and I felt pretty good. I exercised a couple times a week, and I thought about exercising even more. I paid some attention to what I ate. I always bought whole-grain bread. I read somewhere that red wine had health benefits.

I was not paying attention when a latent gene kicked in and the time-to-detonation clock started ticking, so complacency did not turn to alarm right then; it was out of sync. I knew that the fact that my father had had his first heart episode in his late forties meant I was also at risk. I knew the possibility of blocked arteries was there, rolled up tight like a seed. Or at least I imagined it was rolled up tight and not already uncurling deadly tendrils into my circulatory system.

Everyone's body breaks down eventually. Still, when I saw ads for statin drugs promising to lower cholesterol, I thought, *Not for me.* I watched the silver-haired couples frolicking on the beach below the pharmaceutical logo, and did not relate. *They are old,* I said silently to myself. *That is the future.*

I didn't say it in words, not even silently, but I almost thought it: *I will live forever.*

2. Indignation. All of a sudden, you're aware of something that didn't happen suddenly at all. But now that you know it, everything is different.

When I got the results from my doctor and saw the numbers, I wondered, *Is this even that bad?*

Then I read the attached note that said: "Your cholesterol is high. It's time to start following a diet low in carbs, and you must limit fats to less than 30 percent of your calories per day." I thought, *Wait a minute. I eat healthier now than I did twenty years ago—when I used to grab a burger and fries in a bag and call it dinner—and my cholesterol wasn't high then. How can this be? I am young!*

I thought, *I cannot believe I even have to entertain the word* cholesterol.

I read the email again and shook my head and whispered, *"How dare you,"* although I'm not sure whether I was talking to the doctor or the cholesterol or myself.

3. Studying. You read up on cholesterol like you're being tested on it, because you are.

I googled "how much cholesterol one egg" and "low cholesterol dinner ideas." Then, because I'm a little competitive, "average cholesterol 45-year-old woman."

I learned to read food labels the way I learned to read poetry: taking time, questioning each component, looking beyond surface appearances. I flipped over every package that shouted, *HEALTHY!* to find out what its insides were made of. When I dissected the nutrition information of an organic, high-protein, low-carb frozen burrito, I saw that it got its shine from various saturated fats, its flavor from enough sodium to keep a person adequately salted for a week. Aha!

I have always loved breakfast—hot things,

cold things, mixing it up every day. It had long been my favorite meal, but as I now knew, it was also a minefield. I discovered on a recipe site that while eggs are cholesterol bombs and store-bought egg substitutes are full of weird chemicals, you could make a scrambled-egg substitute at home using mung beans and eight other ingredients. "SO EASY," the site said. There were just nine steps.

For years, I had added yogurt to my morning smoothies for protein, and also for calcium to prevent osteoporosis, but then I realized that dairy contained cholesterol. I'd rather not have had to choose between my skeleton and my heart, but if it was a choice, I picked heart. So I looked up "protein powder." I had to find plant-based protein, because that was the theme of the low-cholesterol lifestyle—plants, plants, plants!—but not a plant that had endocrine-disrupting properties or one that somehow bound itself to something else and increased my risk for breast cancer, which apparently some plants did. For the life of me, I couldn't figure out whether soy was panacea or poison.

I spent $64 on a bag of flaxseed meal plus two different kinds of protein powder—a vanilla-flavored powder made from peas, and a flavorless whey powder because although whey comes from milk and all the cholesterol sites said don't eat dairy, they also said whey protein could lower cholesterol. When the box arrived, I ripped it open and lined the bags up next to the kitchen sink. I wanted to try them all immediately.

It was challenging, invigorating, all this learning. Look at all the things I could buy to solve the problem! Behold how well I could protect my own heart, how much control I could take of this situation.

4. Anger. This phase is exactly what it sounds like.

I found an overnight oats recipe on a blog dedicated to heart-healthy living. I had the ingredients in my pantry, so I mixed up a jar and stuck it in the fridge before bed, then got up and ate it the next morning. It was thick, creamy, satisfying.

Just so I knew how many fats and calories and carbs and fibers and whatnot I had left to eat that day, I did the math on the overnight oats I had just eaten, using a calculator to get the fractions right. On a notepad, I drew three lines to divide the page into four columns, writing down how many grams of everything was in the oats, the almond milk, the chia seeds, and the spoonful of almond butter. I added it up and saw that it accounted for two-thirds of the fat I was supposed to have in a day. What the hell? Now what was I supposed to do for lunch and dinner?

I ruled out the overnight oats.

I was sick of smoothies.

I never made the complicated egg substitute. Bean eggs were bullshit.

The next day I made a new plan: avocado toast! First, I consulted the nutrition panel on the package of bread, the kind made out of what tasted like ancient gravel and the fossilized bones of someone named Ezekiel. All the websites said avocado was heart-healthy, but when I added it up the proportion of fats wasn't right. Should I have used a quarter of an avocado instead of a half? I calculated again. Sonofabitch.

I was hungry.

I could not believe I had to do a fucking calculus problem every time I wanted to eat. I thought, *Cholesterol is ruining my life with all this goddamn math.*

I realized I had been cursing more lately. Maybe too much.

5. Fatigue. It's too hard.

I decided to eat a bowl of Cheerios every morning instead, because the box (both its front and its side panel) said it contained cholesterol-lowering fiber. I couldn't figure out whether it was okay to pour milk on it. I spooned dry cereal into my mouth and chewed. Lunchtime came and I ate Cheerios again. This was my life now. Everything was oat dust.

A week or two later, I experienced a brief flare-up of rebellion: I had put in the work. I had eaten all those Cheerios. That should have been enough! I ordered pizza on a Sunday night. Monday, I ate one of the leftover donuts someone had brought into the house over the weekend. Tuesday I went to the grocery store hungry and bought a frozen bag of pre-fried mozzarella sticks. They tasted like sand-encrusted rubber, but I ate them because I had unleashed my repressed craving for hot, salty oil and I had to have it.

Wednesday, my hands were so puffy, it ached to make a fist. My ring finger looked like a hot dog wearing a belt.

Back to fatigue.

6. Acceptance. Months pass, and you settle into a routine. It is easier to comply than to struggle.

I was still doing math every day, but not in precise, written-down equations— more general, mental math, rounding up and rounding down. I rotated among a few low-cholesterol breakfasts, including the cereal, which I now ate with a splash of skim milk. I had lunch at home usually, an egg white omelet or a quarter of an avocado smashed on gravel bread or a salad made with vegetables and chickpeas or occasionally, really only rarely, a grilled cheese sandwich. I didn't have wine with dinner most of the time, because alcohol raises blood sugar, and pretty soon I was going to have to go back and get my cholesterol tested again, and they would also test my blood sugar because they always did, and I didn't want any more surprises.

I drank so much water. Every morning I put a pitcher in the refrigerator to get nice and cold. Sometimes I threw in a few slices of lemon and cucumber to make it taste vaguely medicinal and self-congratulatory. People on the internet called this *spa water,* but I thought of it as *smug water.* I guzzled smug water from morning through afternoon, and I hated to admit it, but on the days when I didn't get around to finishing the pitcher, I could feel the lack.

My birthday came along. My family ordered in dinner—tacos, chips, and queso, my favorites. I dipped a chip in hot melted cheese, and it was pure heaven. But as I swallowed, I wondered, *Would this be a brick in the wall of a clogged artery?* I had one more chip, dripping with glossy white glory, and then I found I didn't want another. Well, I did—I wanted it—but I didn't want the worry. It didn't feel worth it.

The next morning, my hands hadn't puffed up quite as much as they used to after a taco dinner. I wiggled my fingers and told myself I reserved the right to have a whole vat of cheese whenever I wanted it, and I would, *I would*. I just didn't want it this time.

I swing back through anger and fatigue from time to time, but I come back to acceptance again and again, because while I might wish to live in a body that doesn't require me to do math before I eat, there's a difference between wishing and thinking. I can either exist in this body or not exist at all, and those are the only two options.

PART THREE

THE SWING

At some point during every visit to my mom's childhood home in Alabama, the adults would send my brother and me out to the backyard for fresh air. When we were very young, the best activities we could come up with were racing my brother's toy cars down the wooden railing of the deck and mashing dandelions into stew with a stick. Then my grandparents had a swing installed, a simple wooden seat suspended from a branch by two rough brown ropes. The swing changed everything.

Given the choice, I would rather have sat in the house with my grandparents than been sent outside to play. I adored my grandparents and always looked forward to these visits to their house. I would gladly spend the afternoon sitting on the tall stool at the end of my grandmother's kitchen counter, watching her whip up bowls of fluffy potatoes in her heavy steel stand mixer. If I could, I would contentedly sit for hours next to her on the sofa, playing with the loose skin on her elbows, clicking my bare fingernails against the shiny mauve lacquered surface of hers, feeling the *zlip zlip zlip* of her quilted polyester housecoat between my thumb and fingers. My grandfather didn't put up with so much touching, but if I sat at the foot of his chair in the den before he headed down the hall for his 7:30 p.m. bedtime I might sneak a lean onto his khaki pants, stained with paint from working on his fishing boat and dirt from picking corn, the industrious puttering of his retirement.

We got to see my grandparents only twice a year, once in the summer on the way to the beach and once during the winter holidays, just for a few days. The clock started ticking the minute we arrived. I wanted every available morsel of their attention, but when I couldn't get that, I'd greedily lay hands on everything in their household—pens, notepads, old porcelain figurines. No wonder they were always sending us outside.

I attribute my inability to share the swing nicely to the feeling that time was always running out at my grandparents' house. Sensing scarcity, I monitored who got what in a way I did not back home. We squabbled about taking turns, not just with our grandparents themselves—we often whined over who got to sit closest to them in the car or at the breakfast table—but with everything, including the swing.

After a great deal of negotiation, my brother and I agreed to alternate swinging in two-minute increments. Neither of us wore a watch then, so to hold the other accountable, we each counted the other's turn out loud, 120 seconds at a time.

"You're counting too fast!" I'd holler. "You skipped a number!" my brother would argue.

One afternoon, after I had counted two minutes' worth of seconds, my brother refused to yield the swing. All of five or six years old, and he had already figured out that a rule is nothing more than an invisible agreement among participating parties. He simply no longer agreed.

"You have to get off now," I yelled from where I waited at the open door between the yard and the garage.

He shook his head, his hands clamped on the ropes as he sailed back and forth over the grass.

"But it's time!"

He stuck his feet out and twirled, his back to me.

It shook my core, his refusal. As if I'd been stepping over sidewalk cracks to prevent the breaking of backs and just realized that it was nothing more than a silly rhyme, I had counted on a fiction.

I was powerless.

It means nothing to invoke an agreement if you're the only one who agreed to it. It means nothing to put in your time waiting for your turn if the other party refuses to keep up their end of the bargain. And it hurts. *I agreed to do this for you, and you were supposed to do the same for me.* Had I the maturity to put my feelings into proper words, that's what I might have said. *I thought we held each other in equal regard, but you didn't treat me like I treated you.*

Nothing leaves you bleeding internally like love being taken away, and that is what I felt: the draining away of time with my beloved grandparents, the lack of consideration from my brother. Not enough love, love running out, love withheld. It was the first time I felt it all at once, and it was my brother who was there as I felt it. So I yelled:

"I hate you."

If I could have gasped at the same time I yelled it—if I could have sucked in an astonished breath at the same time I screamed out that awful sentence—I would have. As I heard the words in the air, those seconds became a snapshot memory. The darkened cave of the garage behind me, the bright backyard ahead, the cool concrete floor under my feet, and the earthy, vegetal smell of potatoes laid out on newspaper at the back of the garage. Standing in the doorway, one hand still suspended in the air after slamming the door so hard the devil himself heard it in hell and bounced it back open, I felt like a missile had blown straight through my body and left a hole, and into the hole poured a sloshing stream of shame.

I was ashamed because what I said was wrong, and I knew it the instant I said it. I loved my brother very much. I still do. I don't get to see him all that often, because we live several hundred miles from each other, but as we grew up I never wished for him to have less of something I wanted more of: love, success, health. He may have been my competition for attention and playthings for a while, but we grew out of that. It wasn't hate I felt, even then—or if it was, it wasn't for my brother.

Too young to articulate it, I was beginning to understand for the first time what would later, in other circumstances, hit me harder: that time was a finite resource. The more time you had in life, if you were lucky, the more opportunities you had to love people and be loved, and then, at a certain point, the tide would turn, and time would start to run out, taking the ones you love with it.

My grandparents have been gone now for a long time. My paternal grandfather died when I was in high school; my maternal grandfather, when I was just out of college. Both grandmothers died within a few weeks of meeting my infant son, their first great-grandchild. It has been ages since I was a girl with a little brother as my chief playmate, the youngest generation in three generations of living family. I have been thinking about my grandparents more in recent years, though, and now I can see why.

It's because that feeling has returned, the sense of looking around to find a target for my anger, something to blame for my unease. I could point to anything or anyone—cholesterol, a rude person at a party, a driver blocking an ambulance—the same way I pointed to my brother and blamed him. But I wasn't mad about the bargain over a swing gone wrong. I was mad, and I still am sometimes, about the bargain gone wrong with time itself.

FRAGMENTS

Information my brain has kept on hand for decades: The chemical formulas for salt (sodium chloride, NaCl) and hydrochloric acid (hydrogen chloride, HCl). The news of a school custodian's death when I was in elementary school, having something to do with his car and the garage and a gas that could kill you even though you couldn't smell it. The fact, learned later, that carbon monoxide is CO.

"There is nothing either good or bad, but thinking makes it so," from *Hamlet*.

Phone numbers I haven't called in years and will never call again.

There are surely countless more important and relevant uses for the brain space occupied by these crumbs. I could use the mental real estate to store my *Washington Post* password, the location of the earrings I hid for safekeeping two years ago and still can't find, or the recipe for the pumpkin bread I've made dozens of times but still have to consult a cookbook to get right. But no. I forget which day is recycling pickup day, and instead remember these tidbits forever. I can only guess my brain is hoarding them like glittery chunks of broken pottery, afraid not to keep them just in case they'll eventually fit together in some kind of mosaic code.

Here's a story that sits nestled among the pieces:

When my mother was a child, a teenage boy lived next door with his family. One night, my grandparents went out and left my mother home with her two brothers, one a year older, one a year younger. At bedtime, she complained to them that she heard a scary noise. They told her to hush up and go to bed. When her parents returned home that night, they found the boy from next door sitting at the top of the stairs inside the garage, hacking away at the interior door to the house with a toy hatchet.

There are holes in that story. How old was my mother? Was she a tiny girl or nearly grown, older or younger than the neighbor boy? If the boy had indeed been whacking their door with a hatchet, how did my mother's brothers not hear it? What was wrong with that boy? And what happened when my grandparents came upon the ax-wielding kid on their dark stairs?

I could ask my mother to fill in these details for me now, but that wouldn't change the pieces I stored in my memory and carried around all my life. No matter what I might learn today about what really happened, this will always be the version embedded in my mind, like a nail in the bark of a growing tree.

Other partial stories I have known so long that I can't remember when I first heard them:

My mother's father worked most of his life for a steel company. On a visit to a coal mine one day, he stood chatting with a group of men as they waited for the mine's elevator to arrive up from the dark underground cavern. When it opened, they saw that they wouldn't all fit—so my grandfather told the rest of the men to go ahead, he'd catch it on the next go-round. As the elevator began to descend, the cable snapped. My grandfather watched as everyone he had just been talking to dropped two hundred feet to their deaths.

According to family legend, my mother's grand-mother—my great-grandmother, whom I never met—was "mean as a snake." After Easter dinner on a sunny April afternoon when my mother was a little girl, she ran outside to play, calling for her favorite backyard pet, a duck she'd named Fluffy. She called and called, but Fluffy didn't come. When she went back inside to report her duck friend missing, her grandmother informed her that Fluffy was the meat they had just eaten for dinner.

When my father was a boy, his parents' best friends—another couple who also had six kids, just like my grandparents did—died in a plane crash. For several weeks after the accident, the deceased couple's children lived in my grandparents' home alongside their own children. It could not possibly have been convenient or easy to have twelve kids in one house, but there was no question that the orphans would stay for as long as it took to make arrangements for them to go live with various family members.

When my parents were newlyweds, before I was born, they were standing in line inside a fast-food restaurant when a child at a nearby table began to choke. The boy's mother was trying to save him by clapping him on the back, but it wasn't working. Frantic, she yelled for help. My father, a medical student, ran over. Holding the boy behind the neck with one hand, he reached into the boy's mouth with his other and swept a finger across his throat, clearing away the bite of hamburger that blocked his airway. The boy coughed and gasped, breathing again, but he also spat out a bit of bloody saliva. My father's fingernails had scraped his throat. The mother, seeing the blood, turned on my father and began screaming obscenities at him.

Which is correct?
(A) Disaster stories were the only stories I overheard as a child. Maybe happy stories aren't

the ones people pass down and repeat because they're not as useful. We think we don't need to remind one another that good things can happen, because we assume everyone starts out with a naive belief in the world's goodness. Instead, we tell tales of warning, the way our ancestors might have told a story about a guy in the next cave over who ate the purple berries that grew on a low shrub and then turned purple himself and keeled over. "Look out," we say. "Don't let this happen to you."

(B) I overheard cheery stories, too—perhaps about someone winning the lottery or being given a lifetime supply of cupcakes or opening their front door one day to find twin puppies waiting for them—but my memory didn't store them.

(C) My memory stored the good-news stories, but at some point in adulthood my brain decided it would be most helpful, in the interest of lending context to current events both global and personal, to remind me of only the disaster stories. To make it so that when I looked back and when I looked forward, all I saw were flashing lights, warning me of trouble.

My mind periodically sifts through these story fragments, packed into my head next to scraps of information and alongside my own memories, in search of something useful. Have I missed something? Has the world been sending me signs all this time?

Why would I have kept them if not to learn from them? But learn what? That the world is full of hatchet-wielding creepers, plummeting elevators, crashing planes, and screaming strangers? That maybe if I had been paying attention, I would have known earlier that you can be oblivious to peril even when it's right there, making no effort to hide. You can be up to your elbows in it, other people might be able to see it, but still, you don't know until *you know*.

If the answer is C, I wonder how long I will be stuck this way, wearing disaster-colored glasses. Every time I pass the ducks who paddle around the pond near my house, will my brain helpfully go, *Remember: It's always possible that someone could cook and eat your pets!* Jesus.

None of these stories were told to me personally, not that I remember anyway, and the remembering is what matters. It wasn't as if anyone said, *Listen. I'd like you to sit down and imagine a child enjoying a Happy Meal. Now picture that child beginning to choke. . . .* I overheard them in adult talk, around the dinner table, usually.

For example: Over alphabet soup and cheese toast, my parents reminisced about a man and woman they were friends with a few years earlier in medical school, a couple who were expecting a baby around the same time my mother was expecting me. I scooped up the noodle letters

154

I needed to spell "hi" in my spoon, as my parents remembered out loud how the woman had developed postpartum psychosis. I filled up another spoonful with broth, leaving out the green beans, as I heard my mom recall how the woman broke the hospital window and jumped to her death and my dad say, ah yes, it was terrible, how when she landed on the concrete below, her leg bones went all the way through the upper half of her body. They shook their heads. My mind opened up a drawer and dropped that story into it—filed under *B* for *bones*—and I finished my dinner.

BOMB SHELTER

Then there's this story, which never came up in all that time.

I was making slaw on a Sunday afternoon a few years ago when my dad called. As I shredded cabbage into thin ribbons on my wooden cutting board, we talked about what Dad was up to that weekend. He had plans to replace some sprinkler heads in the front yard; then he was going down to the car dealerships to test-drive the latest models just for fun; then he was going to buy a ticket to watch a sci-fi movie my mom didn't want to see. Just as the conversation wound down and I was about to say goodbye, he remembered he had a question.

"Oh, can you get a book for me?" He was perfectly capable of ordering his own books, but in my years working for a bookstore I had begged him to order from indie shops instead of from mega-retailers online. Now he often asked me to obtain books he wanted from the store, just to show he was down with shopping local. "It's called *Raven Rock*."

Having heard some buzz about Garrett M. Graff's book when it came out, I knew it was the true story of the secret underground bunkers maintained for decades during the twentieth century, intended to house and protect high-ranking government officials in the event of a nuclear attack. The book's subtitle says it all: *The Story of the U.S. Government's Secret Plan to Save Itself—While the Rest of Us Die.*

My father had dedicated his life to intellectual challenge and scientific innovation. He traveled the world to teach and learn from other surgeons, sharing expertise in his highly specialized field of neuro-otology. When he couldn't find the exact tools he wanted for performing microsurgery inside people's ears, he invented them. He also created and patented his own versions of tiny prosthetic ear bones. On weekends, he prowled Home Depot for tidbits of metal and plastic, screws and hinges, then put them together and took them apart in his basement workshop, creating prototypes for things he'd like to make on a smaller scale. His work was as sophisticated as it gets, using cutting-edge equipment to restore people's hearing and relieve patients of pain. He operated on the insides of people's heads with lasers.

But when it came to literature, his taste was less scientific, more fantastical. Give him the wildest science fiction, the most bizarre true stories, and the most outlandish alternative histories and he was a happy man. His bedside table was stacked with paperback novels about what the world would be like if the planet were ruled by Russian robots or if America had been taken over by zombies.

When he asked if I'd order him this book about hidden subterranean government control centers, I said, "Sure, Dad. Sounds right up your alley."

"Oh yeah. It reminds me of when I worked there."

"Worked where?"

"There."

". . . there?"

"Yeah, at Site R—at Raven Rock."

Oh, of course. *There.* The secret underground bunker he had never mentioned to me once in my life.

You think you know somebody.

As I processed what my dad had told me, it reminded me of an evening just weeks before, when I sat cross-legged on the floor of my bedroom, three balled-up pairs of socks on the rug before me. John walked in and said, "Laundry?"

"No, I'm learning to juggle," I answered. I had tried to start with tennis balls, but I'd had to backtrack to something softer. "The third ball just won't stay in the air."

"Here." He picked up the three sock balls, bounced them in his hand for a few seconds, and then, just as casually as if he were loading forks into the dishwasher or hanging up a soggy bathing suit, he tossed one sock ball high in the air, then another, and then another, until all three were arcing high, one over the other. This was no beginner's luck. He was zinging these things around expertly and fast, like a sideshow performer.

I couldn't stop laughing. "Are you kidding me? You can *juggle?*" It was like I had accidentally fallen against a hollow wall that gave way to a secret room. We'd been married twenty years, and I had no idea.

If something like that could elude me about the person I'd lived with for two decades, there could certainly be whopping surprises from the people I lived with for the two decades before that, too.

My mother and father were both born within a year of the Soviet Union detonating its first nuclear device at a remote test site in 1949. They began attending school during the early 1950s, when children were routinely shown the educational *Duck and Cover* film made by the Federal Civil Defense Administration. The short movie—in which the narrator warns, "The bomb could explode any time of the year, day or night . . . We hope it never comes, but we must get ready"—included an animated sequence starring a character named Bert the Turtle. You might not have a built-in shelter like Bert's shell, the film advised, but you can still take cover in the event of an atomic bomb, even if it's just by crawling under your desk! (Cue the upbeat music.) Two more decades of the Cold War passed as my mom and dad grew up, met each other in college, and married. By the time they became parents during the post-Nixon 1970s, the big question posed during their childhoods still loomed: Who would push which button to annihilate whom, and when?

When I called to ask my mother what she remembered of that time, she said that we lived near Fort Ritchie, which I knew, in what she described as "a tiny community of army nerds with very specific training." The life had its perks, she said. My parents were invited to have lunch at the White House. My mom fondly remembered "the guys from Camp David" who visited her in the Hagerstown hospital where my brother was born.

Is it really possible that I had no idea what my dad had been doing until so recently?

I did recall having a vague sense, growing up, that my dad had been involved in something unusual when I was a baby. I knew we had lived near the nation's capital during the Bicentennial Celebration of 1976, because I'd seen pictures of my toddler self walking around the parade grounds waving a little American flag. I had seen my dad's big pewter Camp David mug on a shelf in his basement workshop, which for years I thought had something to do with my uncle

David—Dad's youngest brother—and, well, summer camp? It's amazing the things you don't question as a child. I didn't know what Camp David actually *was* until elementary school, and then I just filled in the blanks: We'd lived near there when my dad was in the army, so he must have visited and gotten a mug. We also had a collection of juice glasses with the Muppets on them from a Burger King kids' meal promotion, but I never suspected my parents had been secretly moonlighting on Sesame Street.

And it wasn't as if our family stopped doing regular things while my father was doing this not-at-all-regular job. I went to nursery school. We planted a garden, and I stepped on a bee. We found a baby bird and tried to feed it in a shoe box and buried it when it died. I found a roll of cinnamon breath mints and ate the whole thing and for one long afternoon thought I could breathe fire. The extraordinary doesn't wipe out the ordinary. People get married during wartime. Babies are born during epidemics. My mom drew water for my bath and flung wet clothes into the dryer and taught me to tie my shoes while my father did test runs for the end of the world.

A few days after my dad dropped this news, I called back again to press for details.

"Okay, so I know you were in the army during Vietnam. That's why you and Mom lived in

Hawaii before I was born." In his first assignment as an army doctor, my father had treated injured soldiers—his peers—flown over from the battle-bloody jungle. He had never imagined war as some kind of vague, far-off possibility. He knew the truth, that whether it is happening here at home or on a continent far enough away to seem "foreign" to those who wish to distance themselves from it, conflict is raging somewhere at any given time. War is always. "But what exactly were you doing when we lived outside DC?"

He explained that he had been a general medical officer stationed at the Fort Ritchie health clinic. He and some other officers were assigned the job of going to Camp David for routine tasks such as giving flu shots to the company of marines stationed there. My dad was not the physician to President Ford—he was far too young then—but he was at Camp David sometimes when Ford visited.

"But what about Raven Rock?"

"We called it Site R. My army corpsman, George, and I would go over fairly frequently to check on things. Sometimes we'd take the Oldsmobile ambulance to the helipad when the secretary of defense came up. Good thing the helicopter never crashed." He chuckled.

"But the thing with the drills, what did you practice?"

"We practiced the plan."

"I know, but . . . what *was* the plan?"

"Well, the plan was, George and I would get over there fast to open up the hospital and hope the rest of the team would get there soon. I suppose we were there to keep people alive—the people who would run the country and the military in the event of a disaster."

"Holy shit, Dad. How did you feel about all that?"

"Dazzled, at first! Then kind of bored. We were never put to use, thank goodness."

Graff's book—which I also bought for myself when I bought Dad's copy—includes a scene in which President Ford's press secretary, Ron Nessen, tours one of the secret bunkers in 1976:

> *The last line of his evacuation instructions had been clear: "There are no provisions for families at the relocation or assembly sites." Would he have really abandoned all of his family in the country's hour of need?*

What a question.

Was it strange for my father? To descend below the surface of the earth, to go through the motions of what he would do if the president were rushed into an underground hospital while, above ground, human life ceased? Did he walk out of our house in the morning as I ate my toaster waffle imagining that if this thing he practiced ever came to be, he would one day walk out of this house and never walk in again? That my mother, our house, my baby brother, and I would all be blasted into hot dust? I asked if the existential weight of it ever got to him.

He handed the phone to my mom.

"Every now and then they would sound the siren," she said. "And off he would go into the cave, and there we would sit at home. I didn't feel like we were in any real danger of having a nuclear attack—it was just drills. But every now and then I would look at you and think, 'Well, what are we? Lunch meat?'"

I wondered whether my dad ever thought the whole exercise was pointless. If humanity has nuked itself into oblivion and there's no safe world left to return to above ground, it's not like hunkering down in a man-made fallout fortress will be any more effective than ducking and covering beneath a desk. The end still awaits whenever they open up that chamber, meaning no one is really saved, only temporarily protected. Getting ready for the bomb to fall doesn't even predict or influence whether the bomb will fall or not. It's all pretend, just busywork, isn't it? What is a bomb shelter but either practice for something that will never happen or a postponement of the inevitable?

Dad didn't want to talk about it anymore, so I stopped asking questions, but only out loud. It was impossible to picture him doing those drills and not ask myself: Would I have done it? Could I have left my family behind in a nuclear holocaust? It's one thing to consider this now, in retrospect, when the thing didn't happen. What-ifs don't mean that much after the fact. But at the time, the "if" was still ahead of them. It could have happened anytime; they didn't know.

The amount of time that elapsed between my two-year-old self toddling along the National Mall waving a flag and my eighteen-year-old self moving into a dorm feels vast to me, but I know now how time moves when you're grown up, and I know those years must have gone much faster for my parents than for me. To my dad, hardly any time at all passed between when the siren called him into the bunker and when he started packing boxes full of shelf-stable food to send to his baby at college.

PART FOUR

TOUGH GIRL

Our daughter sat in the dark behind her closed bedroom door, eyes open, ears alert, as we yelled:

"Now."

"Now."

"Now."

"Now."

We did not know she was awake.

She would turn thirteen in a few days. Three years younger than her brother, she had already heard plenty about adolescence. As he had entered his early high school years, we had tried to help her adjust to his growing up the same way we had once helped him, as a toddler, accept her presence as a baby.

Back then, we had prepped him for her arrival—and for the reality that a new baby would require attention that used to be dedicated only to him—by creating a call-and-response game. "What do babies do?" we'd sing, and then we'd answer ourselves, "They cry!" Once we brought her home, whenever her baby-kitten mewling rose to a hearty squall, we'd smile big and go into our routine: "What do babies do?" He, knowing his part, would reply with gusto, "They cry!"

"Good job, baby!" we'd cheer together.

A decade later, when his moods fell prey to adolescent hormones, we said to her, "What do teenagers do? They argue!" Sure, teenagers don't always argue, just like babies don't always cry. But we wanted her to understand that he was only doing the age-appropriate job of a teenager by pulling away from us and asserting his independence. We had new questions to navigate: where he could and could not go and with whom; where it was acceptable (to him) to be dropped off and when it was acceptable (to us) to come home; and why one must look one's parents in the eyes when they're talking instead of at one's phone. There might be a bit more quarreling around the house for a while, some issues that would demand Mom and Dad's time—but it was just a life stage. Normal, if exhausting.

Once, after witnessing a typical parent-son kerfuffle—probably something about leaving the back door open and letting mosquitoes into the house again—she asked, "Will I argue when I am a teenager?" She was about ten years old. We laughed and said, "Yes, you will, and we will still love you." We could see her wheels turning, how she seemed determined to find a way around the inevitable conflict, to be a teenager one day without all the raised voices.

I can't pinpoint a single first memory of her wheezing, but I know it was early. We have pictures of her at four, sitting on the pediatrician's paper-covered table in green polka-dotted leggings, hooked up to a nebulizer for a breathing treatment, bathing her lungs in a cool, soothing mist. Whenever a cold germ made it into our household—which was frequently, as it is in all homes with young schoolchildren—three of us sniffled and sneezed for a few days, but it seemed the fourth, our girl, always fell harder, as if she'd caught a worse version of what the rest of us had. Her lungs filled up and she coughed throughout the night. We turned the television on, hoping Big Bird might distract her, as if her cough might go away if she just forgot about it for a few minutes. She lay on her blanket pallet on the sofa, surrounded by boxes of tissues, jars of VapoRub, and mugs of warm apple juice, and I lay behind her, feeling the muscles of her back work with every labored breath. I inhaled slowly and exhaled smoothly, trying to will her breaths to sync to mine, as if I might use my lungs to breathe for her.

At first it seemed as if she just never fully recovered between colds, but by the time she began first grade, we figured out that the ever-present purple half-moons under her eyes were actually symptoms of allergies. A miserable test—during which I had to hold her down while a nurse pricked her back with dozens of needles—proved she was allergic to a long list of grasses, trees, and pollens. No wonder she was sick all the time. I was constantly pushing the kids out the back door, saying, "Get some fresh air!"

She started getting allergy shots twice a week, acclimating to the sharp jabs quickly, impressing the nurses when she'd strut up to the shot lab for her turn, pushing aside the ruffled sleeves of her T-shirt to expose her tiny biceps. She always refused their offer of an ice pack. "Tough girl!" they'd crow.

The shots barely took the edge off the allergies, though, and year after year she spent much of spring, summer, and fall holed up inside, toting around a grocery sack full of tissues—her snot bag, as she and her brother called it. "I hate spring," she'd say every April, her words bubbling up through mucus.

But that was the extent of her complaining. When she couldn't breathe—when we'd been listening to her try to sleep for hours, counting breaths she was able to take between coughs, bringing her into our bathroom to inhale steam from the shower, and watching to see if the skin between her ribs stretched tight with each breath—we'd call the nurse advice line at the children's hospital and they'd ask to listen to her. She always sat still and wheezed into the receiver as we held up the phone. Even when they said, "You better bring her in," she didn't fuss.

She seemed determined not to be any trouble.

When we finally purchased a nebulizer to keep at home, she sat at the kitchen table and doodled in her coloring book while waiting out the twelve-minute treatments. Made especially for small faces, the plastic mask that attached to the machine had cartoon eyes and gills. We called it Fishy Face, as in, "Come sit down, it's time for Fishy Face." She never dragged her feet or stomped and screamed, "No!" She climbed into her chair and lifted her chin so I could strap the elastic loop around her silky hair and over her ears, cupping the mask over her mouth and nose. I would break open a capsule of albuterol, drop it into the chamber of the machine, and watch as her mask filled with white vapor. It was an eerie sight, this tiny dandelion fluff of a girl coloring with crayons while hooked up to a motorized gas mask, but again, we smiled big. We trained her to look at our faces and trust that all of this was okay. It would only be a problem if we told you it was a problem, baby.

When John called me at the hospital after our son's seizure to report that he had dropped our daughter off at middle school and was on his way, he said, "She was awake."

I didn't understand at first. "What?"

He told me that when he tiptoed into her room to awaken her at 6:30, she was sitting cross-legged on her bed in the first hint of dawn light, wide-eyed. "You're up?" he asked. She said, "I've been up this whole time."

She was awake. Yes, it made sense. How could she have slept through the thuds, the running, the yelling? And then the lights outside her window, the men stomping up the stairs, the loud voices?

John said that when he asked her why she hadn't gotten up and opened her door, she answered, "I was waiting for someone to tell me I should come out."

Because my son is my first child, I learn all the first-timer lessons with him. My first time learning how to change a diaper on the seat of a car, my first time guessing at how to pack a lunch a kindergartner will eat, my first time figuring out how to set up playdates with other kids' parents. My first, eventually, to leave home. Every first overwhelms, at least for a while, until it's no longer new and does not inspire so much confusion, discussion, and adjustment. The unfamiliar necessarily takes up more time, more focus.

I don't need to process as many firsts with my daughter, because by the time she reaches a new life phase, chances are it's not an entirely new parenting stage for me—I have had at least some practice. But the fact that I don't have to spend as much time figuring out every step doesn't mean I care about the steps less. It doesn't mean I protect her less.

If anything, I protect her more.

I have felt protective of her since before she took her first breath, back when I used to watch the ultrasound technician's face carefully at every prenatal appointment; when the doctor recommended bed rest and said, "Be very still"; when I learned that the fact of my body is not, simply by its existence, enough to protect my child and she was born a month early. Like so many mothers do in this age of interventional fertility medicine, I have the sense that this child and I survived something together. I talk less about her when chatting with friends about the ups and downs of parenting, not because there's less to say, but because I'm afraid to rouse the fates. I shouldn't draw attention to the fact that she made it. *She's here, shhhh.*

And she is my girl. The world thinks it has a right to girls. Teachers expect their compliance more than they expect it from boys. Dress codes are designed around what girls should and shouldn't reveal to their classmates. When girls grow into women, governments legislate what they can and can't do with their bodies. People look at girls and think, *What have you got for me? What part of you can I use?*—or *What part of you should I shut down?* I don't want to facilitate that grabbiness, so I find myself guarding her privacy in conversation, even more than I guard his, as if I'm standing in front of her saying, *You'll have to go through me first, bucko.*

Plus, she is a performer. Around the same time she graduated from the nebulizer to a pocket-size inhaler, she tried out for her first school play. She was cast as a singing teacup in a school production of *Beauty and the Beast*, then, over time, as the sassy bird sidekick in *The Lion King*, a comic starlet in *Singin' in the Rain*, the genie in *Aladdin*—larger-than-life characters I never would have had the guts to inhabit, much less at an age when most kids just want to fit in with the crowd. I watch her in every show. She belts out a song while flying in a harness, and I hold my breath. She dances in front of three hundred people while operating a puppet or doing magic tricks, and I am floored. She cries on cue, and when she gazes out past the lights at something she has imagined into being and that none of the rest of us can see I want to stand up, turn around, and yell to the audience, *You may have bought this performance with a ticket, but* she *is not yours.* Of course, she isn't mine either.

People think that if someone reveals a part of herself, they are entitled to all the other parts, too. At a certain level of creative success, the artist becomes a product people buy. They want their actor to look how they desire her to look, their singer to behave how they like her to behave, their movie star to embody whatever character they most want to see. They devour details about her personal life as if everything about her exists for their amusement. My daughter, not even grown-up yet, already gives so much to her audience. I want to make sure she always keeps her soul for herself, that she never believes it's her purpose to be what others want her to be. I guard her, at least in my mind, perhaps more than I guard anyone.

It horrified me to realize I hadn't thought to check on her that early morning. She had sat scared and silent, thinking that's what we most wanted from her.

After our son had rested for a couple of days and when it was time for him to return to school, I found a first-aid video on an educational site about what to do if you're with someone when they have a seizure. I figured he should have something to show his classmates and teammates, to get them easily up to speed on protocol. It occurred to me that our daughter should watch it, too. What if the two of them were in line at the donut shop and he hit the floor? So I pulled up the video on my laptop one morning at the kitchen table and called her over.

She glanced at my screen, then said, "Oh, I've seen that."

She had already watched it a dozen times. She was getting ready, in case it was ever her job to take care of her brother in a crowd where no one else knew what to do.

For years, I'd been looking in her direction, sure that because of her asthma, she was the one most in danger, but it was her brother whose body was brewing trouble. And on that morning of shock and chaos, after the lightning struck in his brain, I looked away from her, toward him.

No one checked on her. No one opened her door to comfort her or explain what she was hearing. She sat there, awake, for over two hours, quietly demanding as little as possible, even though she had to have been frightened. Somehow, despite my best intentions, we had allowed her to think that's what the family expected of her. She performed the role she thought we wanted her to play.

There's an almost inevitable failure built into caring for two people during a moment when one is in crisis and one is not. Because while you may love those people equally, with a fierceness unique to each, you must throw your arms out to catch the one who is falling, and that means you're not there to catch the other, should they fall, too.

Later that week, John and I tried to correct at least some of our failings. We told her: You don't have to stay put and wait for someone to tell you there's a problem. Trust your senses. If you hear a crash, get up. If you smell smoke, get out. You do not owe anyone your stillness or silence, not even us.

WORST-CASE SCENARIO

When our kids were babies, John worked for an international company that required him to travel all over the world. As our daughter was learning to walk, she would often crawl over to my desk, pull up to cruise along its edge, and search the computer screen for her father's face: "Dada?" As far as she knew, he was as likely to appear in a video chat window as to walk through the front door of our house. We used to joke that if he could just set up a meeting with some penguins in Antarctica, he'd have all the continents and could yell *bingo*.

Sometimes he went to a Middle Eastern country that had been embroiled in a bloody war for so long with its neighbor that to enter this country, he had to use a duplicate passport—not his regular one, which included stamps from their enemy. On one trip, airport security flagged him and pulled him out of line. Guards escorted him to a room and ordered him to strip down to his boxers, socks, and undershirt. They took apart his computer and searched his bags, then let him get dressed and packed again, but stationed a guard by his side in the terminal until his flight departed. He never knew why.

(At this point, I feel I should point out that

John is not now and was not then a spy. People always thought he was, but he worked for a software company. Though I guess "he worked for a software company" is exactly what someone would say if they had no idea their spouse was a spy.)

Before a particularly long trip that would send him circling the globe, John handed me a card with a phone number on it. "What's this?" I asked.

"It's to call if anything happens to me," he said.

"But how will I know if something has happened to you unless it has already happened?"

"If something happens, they'll be working on getting me out. You can call to find out what's going on."

It was the phone number for an extraction company. I looked it up and saw that its services were booked by companies whose employees moved in and out of countries with unstable governments. Among its specialties were "field rescue" and "kidnap negotiation and recovery."

One afternoon, I showed the card to a friend while we were out walking our toddlers in strollers around the neighborhood.

"Does anyone ever need this?" she asked.

"I bet they do," I said.

I admit to being a worrier, but it's not like I lie awake at night worrying about what to do in an alien invasion. I only worry about things that could actually happen.

When I was in kindergarten, I watched evening news footage of Mount Saint Helens erupting in Washington. A massive plume of ash filled the sky—it looked like a monstrous gray head of living, breathing broccoli—unleashing more energy than every bomb dropped during World War II combined. But I went to bed that night and slept soundly, without having nightmares about lava or developing the beginnings of a volcano phobia.

We are not born knowing how to sort the events of the world into those we should worry about and those we can dismiss. We have to learn how to divvy these things up. Because young children are constantly experiencing things for the first time, everything that happens is at least a little bit of a shock. As far as I could tell, knowing what to freak out about boiled down to two things: repetition and proximity. If a bad thing happened a lot, or if it happened nearby, it required attention. The volcano had erupted across the country from me, and grown-ups seemed amazed by it. Therefore, I felt volcanoes, a faraway rarity, could safely be put out of my mind as interesting and unfortunate, but not worrisome to me personally.

I don't remember the first time I saw either a fictional depiction or news footage of one human being shooting another—which probably means I was very young when it happened. Given my earliest TV diet, the first shooting I ever witnessed on-screen was likely a cartoon, Yosemite Sam popping off his pistols at a varmint. By the time I started school, I knew gun violence was common in real life, too. I wrote an entry in my first-grade handwriting notebook about the shooting death of John Lennon, as well as a letter, never sent, to President Reagan, wishing him a speedy recovery after the attempt on his life. I heard rumors about a neighbor child who took a gun to show-and-tell and accidentally shot his teacher. Shootings required attention: They were repeated and close.

A hardening happens to human souls as we come to accept terrible things as normal. It protects us the way callouses grow to protect our tender heels as we change from roly-poly babies into upright people whose feet carry the full weight of our bodies. Imagine if we had no hardness—we would feel the full injury and terror of every loss and every threat to every living thing, great and small. Sometimes I wonder if I'm such a worrier because the tough outer shell around the softness of my soul never hardened all the way up.

As a child, I was learning to sort out which things to worry about: a squirrel dashing out in front of a car, a dropped ice-cream cone, a cartoon roadrunner tied to a bundle of Acme explosives, two seconds of a stabbing scene I wasn't supposed to see when I wandered into the den while my parents were watching a movie, diseases diseases diseases so many diseases, a space shuttle blowing up on live television while my friends and I all watched. The shuttle had a teacher on board, a woman who taught kids just like my classmates and me, and that similarity made the explosion feel close even though it was far away. I spent some time considering it— would I go to space if asked? Would I know what to do if a fire started in my space capsule?— before shelving it as an unlikely possibility.

That's how I was thinking back then, figuring out which situations warranted immediate alarm and which ones were indeed horrible but, because of how many other alarming situations there were, could be downgraded to less urgent. Which ones are the most *real?* Guns, yes. Accidents, yes. Fire, yes. Kidnapping?

In August of 1981, just as I was starting second grade in Memphis, Tennessee, the abduction and murder of six-year-old Adam Walsh lit the fuse of every parent's worst fear. Reporters held the nation enthralled with daily updates on the story, airing teary pleas from Adam's mother and father. Crime experts reminded viewers that Adam's mom had turned away from him for only a few minutes—a brief but fateful lapse in attention!—

in the Florida mall from which he disappeared. After the boy's partial remains were found, when there was nothing left to report, Hollywood made a movie about it and put it on television so America could watch the horror acted out all over again.

The spotlight on this and a few other cases of abduction by strangers ignited nationwide paranoia. If you consumed any media at all in the early '80s, you'd think kids were getting snatched and killed by strangers all the time. In fact, later studies revealed that the concept of "stranger danger" was blown wildly out of proportion. Statistics now show that there was no actual uptick in abductions by strangers—that most of the time, missing children were and are taken by family members or people they know. In retrospect, we think today that people were wrong, even silly, to have been so preoccupied with kidnapping. It simply wasn't as significant a threat as everyone made it out to be.

Except when it was.

Three months after Adam Walsh disappeared, a fifteen-year-old high school student in Memphis was kidnapped. Every kid in my neighborhood who could eavesdrop on an adult conversation knew stranger danger was real.

Information filtered through snippets of overheard news reports and rumors passed down to younger siblings from older sisters and brothers who knew the girl—or knew someone who knew someone who knew her—like a ghost story, but true. As children do, the youngest of us processed it through play. At recess, my classmates and I took to the wooded grounds of our school to rewrite our nightmares as triumphant journeys in which we were the heroes. The rules of the game we called Kidnapper were simple: Someone would be "kidnapped" (placed behind a tree and told to sit down), and the rest of us would chase the "kidnapper" (some poor soul assigned to run around and dodge capture), while the victim waited for her opportunity to dash across the pine needles to freedom and touch another tree designated as home base.

We all knew one thing—that a girl from a neighboring school was missing—but none of us knew much more. I did not know, until years afterward anyway, that she had been awakened and taken from her bed at knifepoint by a man who broke into her home. At some point that school year we came to know that several weeks after she went missing, people started finding notes, supposedly written by her, around the church her family attended—in bathrooms, stuffed into Bibles, tucked into desks. We did not know specifically what the notes said, but when we played Kidnapper, we yelled phrases much like the ones scrawled in pencil on those scraps of paper: "Please! This is not a joke!" and "I am alive! I have been kidnapped!" and "Help me! Hurry!"

I imagined the notes had been dropped down somehow from the church attic. My own school was attached to a different church a couple of miles away, where alongside hundreds of girls lined up neatly on slick wooden pews, I memorized Episcopal prayers in morning chapel. I pictured her church looking the same as mine but was fuzzy on the logistics. Were there holes in the ceiling? Could you fly a note through air ducts like a paper airplane? I had seen *The Hunchback of Notre Dame*. I knew, therefore, that there were shadowy individuals lurking in places of worship who, in certain circumstances, might grab someone and take them up to the bell tower. My family often passed the church where the notes were found—it was on the route we traveled from home to school to grocery store— and I checked: It did have a bell tower. I felt I could corroborate what we were hearing through the rumor mill. It all added up.

When police searched her church, they found no sign of the missing teenager. Common wisdom held that the notes were some kind of cruel hoax, created by ghoulish pranksters.

I keep mentioning television.

Remember: There was no internet in the 1980s. What a child knew of the world was what immediately surrounded her in real life—her own family, friends, school, and home—and what glimpses she could get of the larger world through available windows. Television filled in the blanks, I thought, in my understanding of life. I had no way of knowing how many blanks remained unfilled or how correct or incorrect was the mental map I drew of the world based on that understanding.

The major TV networks at the time all aired some version of melodramatic afternoon programming for teens. ABC called its afternoon movie series *After School Specials*, and CBS called their version *Schoolbreak*. NBC went with *Special Treat*, which, given the content of these shows, strikes me now as darkly comic. I rarely managed to watch one of these programs in its entirety because I wasn't allowed to turn on the television during homework time, but occasionally I'd sneak a half hour. They ranged from mild domestic drama, like "Divorced Kids' Blues," to more sensational stories, such as "Are You My Mother?," in which a girl finds out the mom she thought was dead is actually alive and in some kind of institution. Then there were episodes like these:

- "One Too Many"—one of several specials about drunk-driving accidents.
- "Don't Touch"—a variation on the theme that

abuse can come at you from any direction: a sitter, a parent, an uncle, a family friend . . . (See also, and I swear I'm not making this up: "Please Don't Hit Me, Mom.")

- "Andrea's Story: A Hitchhiking Tragedy"—What happened to Andrea when she accepted a ride from a stranger? Well, it wasn't good at all, I can tell you that.
- "A Very Delicate Matter"—Guess what? The matter is gonorrhea.
- "Tattle: When to Tell on a Friend"—Answer: as soon as you notice their interest in cocaine.
- "No Greater Gift"—Two dying boys become friends while hospitalized. Before one dies of a brain tumor, he pledges to give his kidneys to the other upon death. This one prompted thoughts such as, would I give someone my kidneys? Would I accept my friend's kidneys if my friend gave them to me? Would I rather have broken kidneys or a brain tumor? What if my kidney-needing friend was dying faster than I was and it wasn't entirely clear that my brain tumor would definitely kill me? Would I go ahead and offer up my kidneys? Maybe I could give one and keep one. But what if my friend needed something I had only one of, like a heart? Would I offer that, knowing there was a chance I might need it back?

You can see how a kid might wonder, *How will I ever be ready for all this?*

Four months passed between the night the girl was stolen, a knife to her throat, and the night she was found alive in a portion of the church attic detectives had missed earlier. Employees around the church had noticed bread and peanut butter missing from the kitchen. The kidnapper was caught in an attempt to find a food thief. The notes had been real.

In my remaining years at that school, I often rolled my eyes up to the ceiling as we sang our psalms, checking for cracks a folded piece of paper might slip through. How do you tell yourself that something isn't to be worried about when you have evidence that it is? How do you say, "Yes, that happened, but it won't happen again," when you know it could?

In an interview decades later, the missing-then-found girl—now grown into a woman with a career and family—discussed how she moved on after her months in captivity. Her life has been good, she said. The worst happened: She was taken. The best happened: She was saved. But her parents never entirely recovered. Whenever she visited their home overnight as an adult, even years and years after the kidnapping, they still peeked into her bedroom at night to make sure she was there. They would never again be the people they were before.

By the time John gave me the card for the extraction company, I was in charge of keeping two tiny, defenseless people alive. I hoped never to need to call that number, and eventually I put the card away, in the drawer of my desk. I couldn't keep looking at it every day, letting it prompt my imagination again and again. A heart can only hold so many hypotheticals.

RESCUE PRACTICE

I was watching a video about how to administer rescue medication to stop a seizure that lasts longer than five minutes. That's the threshold for emergency intervention. Under five minutes, no big deal; but over five minutes and you're into "status epilepticus," a state of prolonged seizure activity that could lead to permanent brain damage or death. The steps of giving the rescue meds were not complicated: attach the needle to the syringe, poke the needle into the vial of medicine, draw up the dose, take the needle off and replace it with a nasal atomizer, spray half the medication up one side of the kid's nose and the other half up the other nostril. That's it.

It was easy, but I wanted to watch and practice until I felt sure I could do it even with my brain in full panic mode. Not that I *would* panic, of course. But just in case. I also needed to make a rescue kit to be kept at school as well as one to be kept in my son's sports bag.

While I was starting the video over to watch it again from the top, my inbox pinged with a new email. It was a notice from the high school to let parents know that students would be participating in a drill later that morning.

"Today's drill is an intruder alert," it began.

Intruder alert means active shooter drill—what else? What other kind of intruder is there? The kind who runs in and stomps on all the test tubes in the science lab just to make a mess? One who barges in and recites Shakespeare on the intercom without permission, managing to yell, *"TO BE OR NOT TO B—"* before being tackled and escorted out? *Intruder* means guns.

In December of the year my daughter turned seven, in a first-grade classroom almost a thousand miles away from her first-grade classroom, children exactly her age—who wore her same size in clothes, who sang the same songs about liberty and justice and amber waves of grain—were gunned down as they huddled behind their teacher in a corner. Six years later, in February of the year my son had his first seizure, at a high school two states away from my son's high school, fourteen teenagers were killed by semiautomatic rifle fire as they tried to run, hide, and protect one another. On so many occasions before and after and in between those two, children bled to death on their school floors.

Back when flash mobs were all the rage, I used to look around whenever I walked into a mall, wondering whether dancers disguised as shoppers might suddenly jump up on benches and start singing. Later, I looked for exits. I wondered, when my children went to movies or school or pretty much anywhere, where they would hide. They were special to me, but they were not *special*. Not bulletproof.

Every time I get an email about an intruder drill, I remember why we have the drills, and often that's all I think about for hours. On this day, I tried to refocus my attention on the task at hand.

So that was our morning: While my son was at school, practicing how to evade a shooter attempting to take his life, I was at home, practicing how to shoot medicine up his nose to save him.

I heard actress Charlize Theron tell Terry Gross on NPR about a violent incident in her childhood, the time when her mother shot and killed her father in an act of self-defense. He had come home drunk and was shooting at his wife and daughter through a closed door, behind which they'd barricaded themselves. Theron spoke of her father's death with sadness and resignation— she wished it hadn't had to happen—but she didn't blame her mother. In fact, she described her mother's actions with calm admiration. "She ended the threat," Theron said.

I want to end the threat.

But I can't.

If I could, I would end all the threats.

Listening to that interview, I thought about parents who have had to kill for their children, and what a god-awful trade that is. They probably didn't start out in life thinking they'd have to kill somebody one day. They might never have touched another living thing in anger. They might faint at the sight of blood. They might believe thou shalt not kill and if thou does, thou is going to hell. But when the moment comes, they will do what costs them their very soul, because that's how much their love is worth.

Anything less than that ought to be pretty easy.

During a checkup, MD asked my son how he'd been feeling emotionally. The medicine he was taking could cause mood disruptions. My son reported that, true to character, he was on a pretty even keel, although he confessed that sometimes he felt angry. Miming the emotion, he shook his fists in the air and growled, *"Grrrrrrrr*—like this."

MD suggested that occasional anger sounded entirely appropriate.

"When I was sixteen," he said, "it felt like every day I realized something else in the world I had no control over—other people, the news, what went on in my house. The thing is, you actually have more control now than you did as a kid, but when you were a child, you were oblivious. You didn't know to feel out of control. Now you know." He shook his fists, *grrrrr*. "That used to make me feel like this, too."

"Yeah," my son sighed.

I piped up: "I feel like that all the time."

When my son got home from school that day, I asked about the drill.

"We just practice," he said.

"But what do you *do?*"

"We push the big table against the door and get behind it. The biggest guys grab chairs to throw."

"Are you one of the biggest guys?"

"No, Mom—I mean the football guys."

I felt relief, although I wasn't sure why. Was it better to be the one throwing chairs or not? Did throwing chairs even help?

In an attempt to convince me to take a multi-vitamin, my mom once told me, "Whatever's going to kill you has already started by the time you're forty." I wish I could forget that sentence.

Just as we all cruise right past our deathday once a year without realizing it (thank you, W. S. Merwin, for planting that thought in my head decades ago with the poem "For the Anniversary of My Death"), what if we've already had a preview of our death without knowing? What if I'm going to die one day in a car accident and the crash I had last year is the last one I'll have before the *last* one I'll have? What if I could have frozen time at the moment of that impact, paused the skid of my tires just long enough to know, *This is how it will go?*

When I remember the seizure on the bathroom floor, I think, *There are people who have seen their children die.* I cannot begin to fathom that experience, no matter how powerful my imagination. But what if I have seen the *way* my son will die? I tell myself often that the seizure wasn't that big a deal. It was a few minutes of electrical activity in his brain, that's all. It doesn't mean death came so close I could feel its breath before it backed away. It doesn't have to mean that at all.

In the seizure video, one actor pretended to save the other by spraying rescue medicine up his nostril. I hit "restart" and watched it again. Again. Again.

I broke the process into steps. *First: unwrap a syringe.* Then I typed up the instructions and printed them three times on card stock: one for home, one for school, one for sports.

I put the instruction cards with the medicine, the syringes, the needles, and the atomizers into three bags.

Then I took everything out of all the bags.

I unwrapped one syringe and one capped needle. I attached the capped needle to the syringe. There, step one was done! I did it again to the other two sets.

Three times, I put the needle-topped syringe, one tiny bottle of medicine, and one nasal atomizer into a small zip-top bag and labeled it "ONE DOSE." I put the small bags into the larger bags with the extra supplies.

I put the bag for home into the medicine cabinet next to the bag that contains my daughter's inhaler, EpiPen, and Benadryl.

I took the bags out of the medicine cabinet.

I got out a marker and labeled one: "EPILEPSY RESCUE KIT."

I labeled the other bag: "ASTHMA/ALLERGY RESCUE KIT."

I looked at the bags. I was ready. Was I?

Is anyone?

HOMESICK AND SPINNING

No one in Los Angeles notices if you stumble around like you're noon drunk. Or at least they don't say anything, which is either sweet or strangely unsympathetic, and I wasn't there long enough to figure out which. I went to California for a book festival and stayed just over twenty-four hours, checking into the hotel at 2 a.m. after a red-eye flight and departing the following morning around 6. When you come and go during those dark hours, it feels like you're slipping in through a wormhole. It's almost like you were never really there.

I was on a book-signing tour to celebrate the release of my last book. This string of visits to literary festivals and bookstores had been intricately choreographed and carefully budgeted, and at the last minute I had almost canceled them all.

It had been only a few months since my son's diagnosis. I was still answering the phone by telling whoever was on the line, "If the neurologist calls I'll have to hang up on you." My son was still struggling with sleep and getting used to the strangeness of having harmless but unpredictable myoclonic spasms in his arms and legs and neck, and my daughter was adjusting to what we had all been through. They both needed to be driven to school and to their various activities and appointments, and while John had rearranged as many of his own work trips as possible, we were still short on transportation, because we had assumed—back when we started making spring plans, in the early winter—that my son would be driving himself around. But now he wasn't. I'd tried neighbors, friends, and sitters. Understandably, no one could commit to picking him up every day from sports practice; none of his teammates lived near us; and John couldn't pick up both kids in two different parts of town at the same time. There were no bus stations near the field where our son practiced, and I didn't feel comfortable yet leaving his transportation up to a different stranger from a rideshare app every afternoon. I couldn't solve the puzzle.

Three weeks before I was due to leave town, I sat cross-legged on our living room floor, my laptop open to my calendar in front of me, and said, "We can't do this. I'll stay home." For twenty-four hours, I tried to wrap my mind around the reality of canceling my trip, practiced how I would explain it on the phone to my editor.

Within days, I'd be able to see how I was overreacting—how tanking this important professional commitment would have been the wrong way to deal with a logistical problem. But in that moment it made sense: If I couldn't get my son to practice, he couldn't play on his team, and if he had to drop the whole season, that was one more thing about this year that was going to go wrong for him. He hadn't complained about any of it—having to pause driving, taking all this new medicine, having to talk to his teachers at school about his body (the horror!). He rolled with everything, took it all with an, "Oh well, okay." To take away this one bit of normalcy—a couple of happy, sweaty hours outside in the afternoons—felt like too much.

The guilt was back, and it was strong.

A few months earlier, the day before the seizure, the kids had been getting ready for winter exams at school. Some of their teachers had taken pity on students who found themselves in an end-of-semester slump (an academic phenomenon with which we are familiar in our house), and had generously offered some simple extra-credit options to help bolster grades and morale. My son's history teacher, for example, told students that if they watched any movie set in a historical era, they could write up a few paragraphs on it and get a bonus quiz grade.

I had tried so hard, for so many years, not to give my children the impression that grades were the point of school. I didn't high-five them for 100s and yell at them for 80s. Rather, I asked questions like, "What do you think went right here?" and "What would you do differently next time?" This was a sensitive subject for me: Having spent decades untangling my own sense of self-worth from tangible proof of success, I didn't want them to think they were more loved when they got an A and less loved when they got a B.

At the same time, it was my job, as their parent, to teach them good work habits, right? If your teacher lets you count watching a movie as a free quiz grade and you watch movies all the time anyway, watching one more is a low-investment, high-reward opportunity. Take it, I told him.

Maybe I shouldn't have weighed in on the assignment at all. I should have said, *Watch a movie or don't watch a movie, whatever,* and let him face the natural consequence of not getting that extra quiz grade if he didn't follow through. It's not like anyone walks around in adulthood bemoaning their sophomore World History grade. It's not like it mattered, in the scheme of things that matter.

The year was almost over. We were very nearly to the part of December when schools give kids back to their parents for a nice long winter break, when we could just be a family and enjoy the holidays. Everyone was tired, and we had all been letting things slip. The house was a mess. Piles of dirty sweatshirts and towels were heaped against the side of the washing machine. We had been ordering takeout more and cooking less, and we were all a little hopped up on candy canes.

All four of us had colds and none of us had been sleeping well, which was making us extra testy with one another. No one had said "thank you" or "please" in several days. We were having a week in which I loved my kids dearly and at the same time wanted to enroll them in a residential program in Siberia. Lately, I'd taken to telling them the story of my c-sections whenever one of them said something rude. They'd huff out of the room, hands over their ears, as I yelled after them, *"And then the surgeon cut through my abdominal wall . . ."*

I was also nervous, as I always was whenever the whole house came down with a cold, knowing that inevitably three of us would recover within a few days and my daughter would stay sick for weeks. One germ would turn into missed school and more missed sleep and wads of snotty tissues everywhere and everyone listening for breathing to turn to wheezing; and if I could just get her better, if I could just pour enough herbal tea into her and turn the cold around, we could avoid that whole situation. If we could just get through the next week of exams and colds and exhaustion, we could make it to Christmas. Over breakfast that Sunday morning, I gave everyone a half pep talk, half scolding about how if we could gut it out and give it our all a little longer, we'd be able to relax so soon. "Let's go, everybody!"

By afternoon, my back hurt like it always does when I'm anxious or tired, my body storing stress around my spine. I was standing in the kitchen, rubbing my fists into my neck muscles, trying to figure out what we'd eat for dinner, when I saw my son lounging in the den, scrolling on his phone. "Did you watch that movie?" I called out.

"Nah," he said, not looking up.

"Are you kidding me?"

I stormed into the den.

"When someone hands you a key to unlock a door, you take it! You don't just stand there and bang your head on the wall instead. I mean, come on, man. You love movies—how hard is this? What did we just talk about at breakfast?" He stared at me as I ratcheted up my tirade to include the whole household: "Does anyone even hear the words that come out of my mouth? Does anyone even *care?*"

With tears in his eyes, he—who almost never yells, almost never cries—yelled back, *"I care,"* and stomped up the stairs to his room, slamming the door.

I could have let it go then, instead of following him up the stairs and planting my feet on the other side of his door. "WE DO NOT RAISE OUR VOICES TO EACH OTHER IN THIS FAMILY," I screamed.

That was the night I lay down on the living room rug. That's when I rested my back and thought about Christmases. I also thought about how much I regretted yelling at my son. I wished it were easier to raise teenagers. I wished I didn't have such a short fuse lately. I wished I were doing a more consistent job handling small rebellions calmly, not taking things personally. I had been navigating so carefully, but I got tired and took my eyes off the road for a second, and look what happened. I screamed at my kid.

A good night's sleep would help, surely. A new day would bring a chance to be better.

I have never forgotten the next morning, the sound at 4 a.m. But that's not the only day I replay in my head. I revisit the day before, too, reaching into the memory like it's a dollhouse and we are the dolls in it, adjusting my body a little this way, my words a little that way. Could anything have happened differently if I had behaved otherwise that day?

The day after I sat on the floor wallowing in guilt, offering up my book tour as a sacrifice to the gods, a sitter agency called me back and said yes, actually, they had someone who could make the drive we needed every evening.

We were saved. I could go!

I had no excuse. I had to go.

• • •

I was a couple of weeks into the tour, having just finished an event in another city, when I boarded the plane to LA. As is my way when tasked with lifting anything heavier than a shoe, I struggled to stow my compact but densely packed hard-shelled suitcase. I was wobbling it into the overhead compartment with both hands when the man in the seat below glanced up and said, "What, you got your whole house in there?" In an award-worthy act of restraint if I do say so, I kept my grip on the case balanced precariously over his head instead of opening my hands and letting go.

When we landed—after I tried and failed to nap on the five-hour flight, and after my ever-so-helpful seat neighbor deplaned—I stood up and tugged the handle of my suitcase. It didn't budge. I pulled harder, finally freeing it from the space in which it had been stuck but making a critical error in anticipating its velocity. As it hurtled over the raised lip of the compartment, it slammed into the side of my head. For a few seconds, I saw stars.

Maybe that's what made me dizzy. Maybe it was lack of sleep. Maybe I'd been eating too much salt on the road and my inner-ear fluids were out of whack. Maybe she's born with it, maybe it's Maybelline. Whatever the cause, when I woke up later, after four hours of sleep under the feather-filled hotel duvet, and turned my head to look at the bedside clock, I felt the room spin. "Wheeeeeee," I said out loud to no one, as the wall went sailing over my bed.

In a way, vertigo is a real hoot. It feels like being tossed around in a clothes dryer, and it comes and goes with no warning. The weirdest part is that it can happen while you're totally still. It looks to anyone else like you're just sitting there, but what no one can see is that you're on an invisible roller coaster. The imbalance your brain perceives feels so real to your body that you can fall right over, as if a giant invisible hand has picked you up and turned you upside down like a salt shaker. The only way to get around—if you have to get around while you have vertigo—is to stay very close to sturdy surfaces. I wall-crawled around my hotel room as I gathered my outfit for the day, washed my body while leaning against the tile of the shower, and propped myself against the bathroom counter with one arm as I tried to dry my hair with the other. When you can no longer count on stability, the key is to grab something solid and hold on for dear life.

Miraculously, the spinning died down by the time I had to catch a shuttle to the event where I was scheduled to speak. I felt almost normal as I slung my plastic name lanyard around my neck, mingled over coffee, and took a seat beside my fellow panelists in front of a roomful of people.

A couple of times as I made my way to and from the hospitality room, I nearly tipped over and had to do a jig, throwing my arms out to the side and grapevining one foot over the other, but my impromptu sidewalk dancing didn't seem to catch anyone's attention.

I always feel off-balance when I travel by myself, although usually not literally. I love some aspects of solo travel, walking along crowded streets with anonymity, alone with my thoughts but with the added entertainment of casual people-watching. I take advantage of having space to myself in hotels and build a fort for my head out of the array of plush, king-size pillows I don't have to share; spread my toiletries out across the whole sink counter; and use that glorious door-tag menu card to order room service breakfast. I fancy myself a real woman of the world when traveling alone, and that bravado carries me through some of the more insecure moments, such as when I'm confused about time zones or feeling carsick in the back seat as an erratic driver rushes me herky-jerky through traffic. Spending a full day at each destination in extrovert mode means meeting interesting people and having fun. It also means burning through my tank of introvert energy faster than usual. I feel capable, proud, and glamorous—and simultaneously vulnerable, lonely, and very tired. And that's *without* vertigo.

After fifteen hours in LA, I had finished the appearance I came for and said goodbye to my colleagues at the festival. Back at the hotel, exhausted and unsettled, I sat on the edge of the bed and yearned for the comfort of my own mattress, my own sheets. I was ready to go home but knew I couldn't leave until the next morning. Then I remembered a restaurant I had passed earlier in the day. When I first saw it, I had paused to admire the colorful patisserie all dolled up in the window: macarons, éclairs, cakes that looked like they were designed to celebrate Marie Antoinette's birthday. Behind them, polished dark wood chairs sat alongside white-marble-topped bistro tables. Light-filled and gleaming, it looked like a Californian interpretation of a Parisian restaurant, one that might be used as a film set.

It reminded me of the time John and I went to Paris for our tenth anniversary. (We had taken separate planes there and back, so one of us would be left in case the other crashed. For the longest time, I thought all couples did this when they traveled.) He had visited the Rodin museum with me twice, so I could see my favorite sculpture—*The Cathedral*, a stone rendering of two people's right hands almost intertwined. We had eaten Berthillon ice cream while sitting on benches shaded by the Cathedral of Notre-Dame.

I got up and followed the comfort of that

memory right out of the hotel and down the street to the Parisian-looking restaurant. An aproned host showed me to a table in the middle of the room, where I ordered a beet and walnut salad, an apple tart, and a martini—not French at all, as drinks go, but a lady two tables over had one and the frost on the glass told me it would be ice-cold, which is the only way I can stand a cocktail, because who wants to drink a beverage the temperature of spit?

When the waiter brought my food, I thanked him and said, "I can't believe I just walked in and got this table." Usually requesting a table for one yields either a stool at the bar or an eight-inch tray-on-legs that abuts the front door so that everyone waiting for their nice roomy booth is standing over me, sneezing on my head.

"Well," he explained, "traffic is light tonight. There was a shooting around the corner. That always hurts the dinner crowd."

"Oh my God! Is everyone okay?"

"Not sure," he said, refilling my water glass from a silver pitcher.

There I was, with my prissy supper, enjoying prime seating made possible by people who canceled their reservations when they heard about a shooting, thinking, *What am I doing here? Who got shot, and why, and who was the shooter, and what did they want, and why is everyone in this restaurant tearing bread apart with their hands and clinking glasses as if one of our fragile fellow humans wasn't just popped like a water balloon by a bullet?*

I was afraid if I drank more than a few sips of the martini I'd ordered, it would make the spinning resume, and I regretted spending money on it just because it looked beautiful and cold. *I want to go home,* I thought. I ate my food, paid my bill, and left.

By the time I returned to the hotel and washed my face, I noticed that if I cut my eyes sharply to one side, the world started somersaulting again. I got in bed and watched a documentary on television, trying to hold my head very still.

The next morning, I used the internet access on my flight to answer emails and check the news. The plane was about to begin its descent into Nashville when I took one last scroll through the headlines and saw the news alert that Notre-Dame was on fire. I tapped my phone to expand the image and saw the spire still standing like a black skeleton against the red blaze that surrounded it, thick rolls of smoke filling the sky. "Oh no," I gasped. I could sense the woman across the aisle from me turning her head toward me; I wondered briefly if she thought something had happened to someone I loved.

My eyes and throat, dry from fatigue and recirculated airplane air, stung as if the cathedral's smoke had crossed an ocean and filled the cabin.

I want to go home, I thought again, which made no sense, because now the plane was landing. I was home. But it wasn't that I wanted to go to a specific location, like France or Tennessee or my own bed.

I wanted to be able to close my eyes and trust that everything and everyone would be how I left them when I opened them again. That walls would hold still, and that we could trust people not to kill one another, and that if a person was about to drop a suitcase someone might put up a hand to steady it. That a magnificent structure that had existed for centuries would exist forevermore.

The kind of "home" I craved was a feeling, not a place. A sense of safety and wholeness, of good intentions and predictable outcomes, or, at the very least, the comfort of togetherness when things fall apart.

THE GREAT FORTUNE
OF ORDINARY SADNESS

I stood at a fruit stand, running my fingers lightly over the fuzzy skin of a peach while willing my bottom lip to stop its ridiculous quiver. I would not cry. A slight change of plans was nothing to be sad about, as sad things go. I knew that.

It was summer. A few weeks prior, I was supposed to have picked up my son after a month at camp on the coast of North Carolina. When I say it's the place he loves more than anywhere else on earth, I mean that every year on his birthday he requests to be woken up with a recording of the camp bugle call, so that for a few not-quite-conscious seconds he will think he is waking up in his cabin bunk. I mean he counts the months, then the weeks, then the days of the school year until he can get back out there. I mean the camp banner hangs on his bedroom door. As of my fruit stand moment, he was a rising high school junior. His plan, ever since he was a young camper, had been to work his way up to the "counselor in training" program—which he was doing for this summer's four-week session—and then, the year after that, to stay and work for the entire summer as a counselor. And then of course, after that, to head off to college with future summers unspooling toward his adult life, away from us.

So I'd been counting on the fact that when he got back from this training session we'd have our final turn to do all the late-summer things we've done as a family since he was born. We'd take our last end-of-summer road trip to visit cousins. Sleep in on our last lazy August mornings. While away our last long, hot afternoons in the quiet of the backyard. This would be our last summer in one place as a family of four, he and his sister together, as they've been all their lives.

But as my husband and I were loading the car to make the drive to retrieve him, our son called from the camp office. There was a last-minute job opening! If he could stay for the rest of the summer, he would be promoted immediately from counselor in training to full-time counselor. He would have his dream job—the one he'd been working toward for years—a whole year sooner than he thought. I've never heard him, or anyone, so thrilled. "Can you believe it?" he asked breathlessly.

I could, but barely. The fact that he was at camp at all still felt like a miracle, like a heist we'd narrowly pulled off. After his seizure in December, weeks had passed in which we had to repeat the reality to ourselves again and again just to reckon with it: This wasn't a onetime fluke, but a condition that could pop up again, anytime, for the rest of his life. He had to get enough sleep. He must never skip a dose of his pills.

That winter felt like one really long day. Or a really long night, to be more accurate. John and I hardly slept. We were exhausted, but our minds wouldn't let us rest, because one night we had gone to bed and slept as our son fell. We had missed our moment to catch him, and if it had happened once, it could happen again. We existed in a constant state of waiting.

Every time we heard the slightest creak in the house, we jumped. Late one night, our son got up to get some water, and as soon as I heard his footfall, without even thinking, I bolted out of bed and sprinted down the hall. "Mom, what are you doing?" He squinted at me in the faint illumination of the hall night-light—both my arms held out ridiculously, as if we were doing a spontaneous midnight trust-fall exercise. He scratched his chest through his T-shirt as he lumbered along to the bathroom.

For John and me, every detail of that early morning was seared into our minds. But our son had no memory of it. He wanted to understand, to remember something, so he kept asking us to describe it to him: What did we hear? What did we see? What was the inside of the ambulance like? We described the scene as best we could—"you were here on the floor, son; this is where we found you"—leaving out the parts no child wants to hear their parents say: *We left our bodies. We bargained with God.*

I did not say, *I knew when I saw your feet that the universe had come to take you from me, and that I had known without really knowing that this was coming.* I didn't mention that the more I remembered, the more I was sure that here on earth my hands may have been dialing 911 and my voice may have been asking for help, but somewhere on another plane I was standing at the mouth of a fiery tunnel, holding my arms out like a shield, pushing back flames with my hands and screaming, NO, STAY BACK, LEAVE HIM HERE. I didn't explain that I went to war with the universe then, that I squared off against Life, which is also Death, that I threw my body between them and him. I remember these scenes like I remember running down the hall, as if they all happened, equally real.

All that is hard to explain to someone so young.

As the holidays ended, school and work resumed, and the calendar's demands began to pile up again. We couldn't stay in our home bubble forever, and we needed to think about what lay ahead. "Oh!" John said one morning in January. "I guess we have to tell camp."

We knew the camp directors were in the

process of evaluating counselor-in-training applications—including our son's—and we thought they should know about this new development. Maybe it would be helpful information to have when placing him in a cabin, we figured. We didn't anticipate that they might write back to say that, actually, their policy is that a child must be seizure-free for one year before they can attend camp, for safety reasons.

"Shit," I said as I read the email. "Shit," John said, too.

Shit.

Not this. Not our son's favorite thing in the world, the place he lived for. He could lose driving privileges; he could lose the possibility of pulling an all-nighter or partying into the wee hours; he could lose the freedom of life without a just-in-case keychain pillbox. But not this. Please, not this. Our boy was once the toddler who, the first time he saw the ocean, seemed to recognize it as some kind of home from a previous life or as the origin of the water in his cells. I had seen my friends' babies yank their little toes back from the cold surf, squint and cry as the salty spray hit their faces, but when I set our son gingerly down on the sand he turned his body to the water and ran toward it with his head thrown back and arms flung wide, mouth open and laughing.

We called MD, who promised to write a letter

explaining that it would take only a few simple modifications—a life jacket, a buddy system—that there was no reason our son couldn't safely participate in the full counselor-in-training experience. The camp leaders considered the letter. We had many, many phone conversations. They met with their medical board. They said they were trying. They said it would be a few weeks. Then a few more.

For two months, our son came home from school every day and asked if we'd had an answer from camp. "Have you heard anything?" he'd ask as he dropped his backpack by the door, and day after day the answer was no. Night after night, John and I lay in bed, listing for each other all we'd give up if we could just exchange something, anything, for this, for him. I have read that a child's illness or traumatic accident can test a marriage, but this whole situation, if anything, brought John and me closer. We may have bickered over who didn't unload the dishwasher (me) or who took the other's nightly cooking for granted (him), but we were united in our wish to trade places with our son or, at the very least, try to salvage the experience that meant the most to him.

In April, the camp directors let us know that they had decided he could come. When we got the email, I was so grateful, I said, "Shit!" again, and raised both fists into the air.

• • •

It was not easy to leave him there, but it would have been harder to see him unable to go. Every day he was at camp, I told myself he would be okay. He would remember his medicine. He would get enough sleep. It was just four weeks, like every summer. It would be fine.

I tried, but failed, not to think about what he had told me in the emergency room, waking up from his postictal hangover.

"Hey," he had said then, looking over from his cranked-up bed, wrapped in the blue blanket. "Remember how I fainted on the last morning of camp?"

I did remember. He had told it as a funny story during the drive back from camp that summer, just four months before our day in the hospital. He had said, laughing, that he had finally joined the fainting club. (I faint all the time. So does my daughter. So does my mom, and so did my grandmother. It's one of our things.)

"What?" I'd said. "You're not a fainter!"

"I know, but I did! I passed out yesterday morning. My counselor found me on the boardwalk between the cabin and the bathroom."

"That's wild! Were you just tired, I guess? Maybe you have low blood pressure, like me."

"Yeah, or maybe I had a stomachache or some-thing. Anyway. It was funny."

There was no reason to be alarmed. It figured

221

that yet another member of the family had inherited the gene for these brief episodes of wooziness. We left the story there, in the car, until he brought it up again in the hospital.

"Mom, I don't think I fainted at camp."

He revisited the memory, and there it all was: He had had a cold all week, which had interrupted his sleep for several nights in a row. Then he had stayed up late to celebrate the last day of the session. He had no memory of actually "fainting," but he knew it happened early in the morning, before everyone else was awake, when he had gotten up to get some water, as is his predawn habit. He knew his counselor had found him, but had no clue how long he may have been lying there. He remembered his cabinmates laughing because he seemed so groggy. They had thought he was out of it because he was tired like they all were after their late night.

"It was all just like this, Mom."

The seizure at home probably wasn't the first seizure after all.

A couple of weeks into his counselor-in-training session, a news story broke about the death of a popular actor, and I learned the term *SUDEP*, which stands for *Sudden Unexpected Death in Epilepsy*. The young man died after having a prolonged seizure in his sleep. I hadn't even known that was possible.

I was grateful that counselor trainees weren't allowed to have cell phones in their cabins, hoping that meant my son couldn't see the news. He and the actor had the same first name.

Now, instead of going to get him back and bring him home, we were just going to spend a handful of hours with him on his day off before he stayed for another month. During our day in the town near camp, we got him a haircut, fed him three meals, and took a spin through Walmart to restock his shampoo and toothpaste. I left his summer reading for school in a zip-top bag on his bunk before we drove away. No more final month of summer together. We wouldn't see him again until two days before eleventh grade started.

"It's almost like you're dropping him off at college," a camp staffer joked, as I signed paperwork in the office.

"Whoa, buddy," I said. Not yet.

Then, so quietly only I could hear it, I added, "I just thought I had more time."

I'm a planner. I had been planning, for example, to enjoy all the nostalgia, pomp, and circumstance over the next ten months as our daughter completed eighth grade, the final year at her childhood school before she and her classmates scattered to various high schools. I had my waterproof mascara and the baby pictures ready for slide shows. I was prepared to help pick out a graduation dress. I was ready to handle her year of lasts. I wasn't ready to realize one of his big lasts was already behind us.

"I thought I had more time" is the refrain of every sudden, tragic loss, but this moment was nowhere near tragic, I understood. Every day, parents lost their children forever to accidents, illnesses, and conflicts that use human lives as bargaining chips. Kids died when diseases overtook their bodies. They died when they were crossing the street. They died when they tried a drug their friends had taken without any problem. They choked on their own vomit after too much alcohol or slipped off a trail while hiking after dark or did nothing at all to put themselves into danger except exist in a world where too many people are both armed and angry.

A parent who has endured the horror of losing a child would give anything to feel this sentimental over a summer gone too soon. Ordinary milestones—such as leaving for camp or college—are only ordinary if they happen. If they don't happen because the chance to reach them has been lost, they are extraordinary. I had it undeservedly and nonsensically good as a parent. What gave me the right to existential fear when so little actually threatened my existence or the existence of my loved ones?

"I thought I had more time." It was pure melodrama for me to claim these words.

Still, I say them a lot. Aren't they also the refrain of most foolish mistakes I make? I have said, "I thought I had more time," after braking too late and hitting a curb. I've said it after missing a deadline, having written down the wrong due date. I've said it hundreds of times after ruining something I'm cooking. How did the water boil away so quickly? When did the muffins catch fire? (The broiler *never* gives me enough time. I should not be allowed to have that setting on my oven.) I am constantly miscalculating.

Speaking of foolish mistakes, how absurd I was to think I had any control over how I'd parcel out my feelings.

It hit me, as we left our son again for August, that I was standing at the beginning of a string of endings, proud and bereft at once. All those years ago, I had taken a leap of faith into being a parent. I had added a little to my life at first, and then more. One baby, then another. Kid stuff, then big-kid stuff. My life had expanded like a balloon to hold the responsibilities, the love, the people themselves, and now I had to figure out how to let them go. My children's leaving—a gradual process that had barely even started— was exactly what any parent would wish for. It's what I had raised them for. And it already felt like my limbs were being pulled off, one by one.

It seems selfish to talk about such a mundane breaking apart in a world where real wreckage lies scattered everywhere. Instead, I try to carry the sadness around quietly, so as not to take up too much air with it, to leave space for the far more significant sadnesses of others. How do we appropriately mourn the passage of time when it's passing beautifully, safely, but not for everyone? And how do we honor milestones that happen while we aren't looking? The first toddling steps, taken at home with the sitter while we're at work, or the first baby tooth, lost at preschool. The last time we saw someone, not knowing it was the last.

All I know to do is acknowledge the fortune of having milestones to celebrate at all. I can celebrate people whose accomplishments mark time in my own life. I can accept that firsts and lasts are both glorious and breathtakingly sad, especially when they sneak up on us. I can watch and listen for losses I can do something about, and then I can stand by someone's side, make a phone call, give my time, cast a vote—anything I can do, as often as possible—to try to make sure fewer parents suffer the unthinkable, that more people will bear only the most ordinary losses.

And I can try to contain my emotions when they hit me like a wave in public, the way they did that late-summer afternoon while shopping for peaches.

If you happen to catch me moping while gazing upon my firstborn's favorite food, know that

I'm pulling myself together. Really, I am. I've just slipped for a second into my own tiny, self-indulgent grief.

And if you, too, are thinking, *I thought I had more time,* for any reason—a loss large or small or so eclipsed by refracted rays of joy that you're ashamed to call it a loss at all—come stand quietly by the fruit with me. We don't even have to talk, unless . . . well, would you mind telling me to turn my oven off? It's so easy to miss the moment when things begin to burn.

CLOSE CALLS

I had planned to call my mother on the evening she turned seventy, but before I found a minute to call her she called me. (It was one year, almost to the day, before the morning on the bathroom floor, but I wasn't measuring time that way. Not yet.) And before I could gather her grandchildren around the phone to bust out an off-key rendition of "Happy Birthday," she sobbed. Unaccustomed to hearing her cry, I thought at first that she was choking.

"Mom! What's happening?"

"Dad's in the hospital."

I was confused. Of course Dad was in the hospital. Dad worked in the hospital. He was a senior member of its medical community, men and women who are not only colleagues but also one another's doctors. The kidney guy treats the orthopedic guy; the ortho guy treats the cancer lady; the cancer lady treats the eye guy. Dad's the ear guy.

She told me she had taken him in to see the heart guy that morning. He'd been having back trouble lately and hadn't been sleeping well, so she hadn't worried much when he had sat up and started fidgeting before dawn. Then he admitted he had been having chest pain along with his back pain. I imagine he got out as much as, *"chest p—"* before my mother grabbed him by the arm and loaded him into the car. She can be cavalier about some things—slap a Band-Aid on it, take an Advil, walk it off—but worst-case scenarios are her time to shine. This is the woman who calls my children before they leave for summer camp to say, "Have fun! Watch for bears! Don't get a flesh-eating amoeba!" I get my keen eye for alarming possibilities from her.

The cardiologist ordered some tests. Dad was lying on a table for one of these procedures when, one after another after another, his coronary arteries collapsed, completely blocked.

"They came running out to get me," my mom cried on the phone. "They put the papers right on him. I signed the consent forms *on his chest*." She broke down trying to describe the sight of my dad on a gurney, being rushed down the hall of the same building where he had operated on someone's inner ear the day before, now headed into emergency triple bypass surgery.

"I'll be there in six hours," I said.

I got off the phone and went to our bedroom, where I scooped a pile of folded laundry from the floor into a black nylon travel bag. I kissed my children on their heads, told them to eat whatever their dad gave them for dinner, and got in my car. Then I drove through the night—over long stretches of highway, around the hairpin turns that twist up and down Tennessee's Cumberland Plateau, and across the state line into Georgia—in hopes of making it to the hospital to see my father alive.

My parents had been married for nearly five decades. John and I had just celebrated twenty years, which made me think we should have at least thirty more. Life's math requires so much subtraction.

I arrived at the hospital in time to see my father awake, still slightly sedated, and very unhappy. My brother, also a doctor, had driven in from three hours away. We took turns sitting in the waiting area and going back to our dad's room with our mom.

Dad's energetic bedside manner had disappeared now that he was the patient. A clear oxygen tube snaked under his nose, and wires ran from between the snaps of his hospital gown up to various monitors. Dad had always composed his daily look carefully: neatly combed hair, seasonal tie featuring pumpkins in October or flags in July, dark leather loafers buffed to a high shine, white doctor's coat laundered in hot water and pressed crisp. True, he also mowed the lawn in black knee socks and khaki shorts. I'm not saying he always made *good* choices, just that the outfits, like other decisions, had always been his to make. Now, sitting under a rumpled sheet, he wore his tortoiseshell-framed glasses, a touch of dignity and style, but his mouth sagged. His colleagues were out in the hall, talking about him, not to him.

A few hours before, I had been wondering, *Will he live?*, but now that I saw him, the most urgent question seemed, "How soon can he get out of here?" His doctors were cautiously optimistic. Dad had survived the surgery, the first important step, and now, if all went well, he would face an uphill climb back to normal. If he continued to stabilize on schedule, he could go home in a few days, but home would have to be turned into a recovery unit. We agreed that my brother would help my mom set up the house while I went home to repack for a longer stay, then I would come back to help manage Dad's care at home with my mom for a week or so.

For the second trip to Georgia a week later, I booked a round-trip flight. I didn't want to arrive already tired from another drive.

My mother deserves a prize for her caretaking skills, not only in a lifetime achievement kind of way but specifically for this period of time. When I arrived, I saw that she had rearranged their house to turn the first-floor den into my dad's recovery suite. She had brought her pillow and blankets down from upstairs so she could sleep on the sofa every night, and by *sleep* I mean lie awake, listening in the dark for my father to stir. She looked tired.

My dad spent most of those days and nights in an enormous maroon recliner my mom ordered. It had a button that would gently tip the chair toward standing when he wanted to get up; when he pushed it, my mom would jump up and stand by, ready to steady him as he got to his feet. She made sure he kept a small cushion handy for holding against his chest when coughing or breathing deeply, which he needed to do regularly to make sure his lungs were clearing out fluid properly. She cleaned his chest incision and watched for signs of infection. She helped him on with his compression socks to prevent swelling in his legs, from which the surgeons had harvested healthy blood vessels. Because he could not lift anything heavier than a couple of pounds, she lifted, pushed, pulled, and dragged whatever needed moving or carrying.

I was there to spell her during the day, to give her a chance to rest and shower without leaving my father unattended. To make myself useful, I chopped carrots and onions and filled their freezer with two-serving portions of soup. I borrowed my mom's car and went to Bed Bath & Beyond, looking for warm slippers with rubbery grip on the bottom for when my dad could get up and walk around again. I had read somewhere that music lifts mood, so I made playlists of their favorite 1950s and '60s music and uploaded them to my dad's phone so he could play them on a speaker the size and shape of a soda can. Dad and I spent hours in the den, him dozing and watching his cable news shows, me answering emails. I was still working for the bookstore then, but as long as I had my computer, I could keep up from anywhere. I could also silently email everyone I knew with a parent who had also had bypass surgery. I lined up their stories in my mind, ranked from worst (their parent died) to best (their parent now skydives for fun), periodically checking Dad's recovery against the spectrum.

The time I spent at my parents' house seemed to vibrate with a constant but dull tension from morning to night and into the next day. It was the kind of time that makes you look for metrics to divide it up and give it structure. How long was I there? Eight breakfasts. Nine blood pressure readings. Six showers. Three trips to the pharmacy.

On our second or third morning, my mother lit her stove top to warm up some lunch but didn't put a pot on the burner. Instead, she washed her hands, dried them on a paper towel, and then discarded the paper towel next to the stove before leaving the room. I happened to walk into the kitchen as she walked out, in time to spot the torch blazing on the counter and knock it into the sink with a metal spoon. Blackened paper sizzled to soggy ash under the faucet.

After almost a week, my dad was starting to sleep well at night, which meant my mother could sleep. A visiting nurse was scheduled to begin daily check-ins, and my brother said he could come in a few days. I felt like it was safe to stick with my plans and take my return flight home.

I did feel guilty about leaving, although I also felt guilty about having been away from home so long. I had missed a chunk of the Christmas season with my kids already. If I stayed much longer, I wouldn't be there to feed them while they studied for exams. I would miss my daughter's holiday concert at school. Her birthday was coming up the week of Christmas, too, and I hadn't even thought about it yet. I had canceled a work event and extended two writing deadlines. I knew everyone at home was fine—John was great at the daily routine—but while he assured me it was no problem for him to take a conference call on speakerphone while sitting in the school parking lot, I also knew he had canceled some meetings that week. If I could just get home for a while, I could catch up and no one would feel like they had missed anything. Not my kids, not my parents, not my colleagues, not John. I could zip up all the gaps.

As I was wedging my travel-size toiletries back into their case that night, my phone lit up with a weather notification: A freak snowstorm was on its way to Georgia. No sooner had I digested that highly unusual news than my phone pinged again. The airline had canceled my flight for the next morning because planes couldn't get in from cities that had already been hit by the blizzard.

One more day. Okay. I could do one more day.

I rebooked my flight for twenty-four hours later, hoping the forecasts might be wrong and the snowy front would turn northward. It didn't. But when I got up and checked my phone, the airline indicated flights were back up and running despite the snow.

I counted the soup containers in my parents' freezer, made sure my dad had his warm slippers on, and made my mother promise she would take a nap in the afternoon before the visiting nurse arrived.

"Call and tell me how the appointment goes, okay?"

"I will, I will," my mom said. She shooed me out the door and into a cab.

In the back seat, I told myself, *They'll be okay.* The nurse was coming this afternoon and tomorrow, and then my brother will come. They won't be alone. I texted John: *On the way to the airport. Will text when I land. Order dinner?*

• • •

I walked through the airport to the security line, dragging my bag like a big blue dog on a leash. The travelers ahead of me in line stripped off their shoes, belts, hats, jackets, and watches. Everyone peeled off their armor to expose their soft inner layers, to prove they were harmless and safe to fly.

The weight of leaving my parents began to hit me, and my eyes welled up when I went into the restroom to wash my hands. Soaping between my fingers under the automated trickle of water, I remembered when my babies were born, how all the hospital room doors bore signs reminding visitors to wash up. I stood between two other women at the sink as we all lathered and rinsed, and thought, *I'm doing this for them, and they're doing this for me, and we're all doing it for each other's parents and kids and friends.* I knew I was being overly sentimental about a crowded airport bathroom. Still, I felt held for a few delusional seconds in the generous embrace of an imaginary world in which we all operated carefully, lovingly, in one another's best interests.

I took shallow breaths, as if the key to holding back tears was not to give them too much oxygen. I felt like a bag of glass shards. Surely, it wasn't just me. Did any other women at the sink also feel this way? I wondered how many travelers were navigating this airport while reeling from something life changing but invisible to everyone else, looking whole but feeling broken.

Lifting my face to the mirror, I was caught off guard by the sight of my watery eyes, red nostrils, and skewed ponytail. Yikes. I *looked* like a bag of glass shards. I glanced quickly away and made the briefest eye contact with the woman next to me in the mirror, then dropped my eyes back down to the sink. Nothing like a person on the verge of a breakdown staring at you in a bathroom mirror while you're trying to reach for some soap. Sorry, lady.

The flight was full, and it boarded on time. I had finished the book I brought and forgotten to charge my laptop, so after I buckled into my seat I closed my eyes and tried to ignore all the jostling about as my fellow passengers loaded up.

Sitting there, I remembered how my mom used to tell the story of being pregnant with me, how she hadn't realized it until well into her second trimester. She had hardly gained any weight and didn't feel at all different until suddenly she did. What a surprise! Her experience was so different from my own. Once it had become clear that there would be no surprises in conceiving my children, I had tracked every micro-movement of every egg, had my blood drawn from my arm into a thin tube every few days to monitor my hormone levels, and injected fertility-assisting drugs into my own thigh and belly for months. (I injected myself because when John had practiced with an empty syringe on an orange—as he was instructed to do at the clinic's "how to support your partner" workshop—he stabbed it so hard the needle broke off. Oops.)

On the night she went into labor, the story goes, my mother thought the spaghetti she had made for dinner had given her indigestion, until the contractions became impossible to mistake for anything else. Even at the very end of her pregnancy, she didn't recognize one phase turning to the next. I, on the other hand, had been watching for signs and calculating their odds of survival before my children even existed. I wondered how much that difference in beginnings affected the kinds of mothers we turned into, or if it did at all.

Departure time came, and the plane didn't take off.

An hour later, we still hadn't moved.

By the time two hours had passed, every passenger was furiously pecking away at a phone, trying to rebook another flight or communicate with someone back home. Nearly forty-eight hours after I had first packed to leave my parents' house and go home, I still wasn't on my way.

We all deplaned, back into the terminal.

• • •

There's a lot I don't recall from that bleary, strange week, but I remember this next moment as if it's happening right now:

I am slumped in a chair next to an airport coffee cart like a rock in a stream, people flowing around me. It's a tiny airport, and there is nowhere to go to get out of this rushing current of humanity. I am hunched over, my forehead on my balled-up hands. Despite my sense all day that a sob was building in my chest, I'm not sobbing. I'm not shaking or making any sound at all. I am dissolving. Too tired to hold in the tears, I am simply liquifying, melting, weeping like a sore weeps. The cell walls have burst.

All I want to do is take care of everyone I love, but I can't do it. I can't be two places at once. I can't even get from one place to the other. My parents might be okay right now, the kids might be okay, John might be okay at this very moment while I'm sitting here, stuck, but eventually something will happen and I won't be there. That's bad enough, knowing that loss is inevitable, but there's another kind of loss wrapped up in this, too. If I want to take care of everyone and tuck them all up under my wing, but it turns out that it's impossible—that there is no such thing as keeping them all safe, that no one can ever get everyone they love under their wing because nobody can be everywhere at one time, no wing is big enough—then my whole goal is rendered moot.

This is worse than just not getting what you want: realizing that the thing you wanted was imaginary, a wish. It's a death of sorts.

Why am I even here? I thought in that airport. *Why try?*

I waited nearly twenty minutes to call my parents and tell them I was stuck. I wanted to compose myself. I didn't want them to hear my voice and think that returning to them was making me upset. It wasn't that, or at least it was so much more complex than that.

I rode quietly in the back seat of another cab, back to my parents' house, and texted John and the kids that I wasn't coming home just yet. I ate dinner with my mom and dad, took out their trash, and put myself to bed.

At 6 the next morning, I checked the airport's status. It was a mess. Too many flights had been canceled or rerouted, and I couldn't get a seat on any plane leaving that day. So I did what I had resolved to do the night before if it came to it. I rented a car online. All I needed to do was get another cab back out to the airport—which, coincidentally and ironically, was also the location of the car rental agency. I might not make it out of there on a plane, but by God

I would depart from that airport one way or another.

When I came downstairs to report my intentions, the plan hit a snag: my mom.

"You can't drive! People are stranded in ditches outside Atlanta!" my mom cried. (I texted a friend in Atlanta. *No one's in a ditch. The roads are fine,* she texted back.)

"I need to go now, Mom."

"No, you have to fly. That's the only safe way. There are flights going out of Columbia. I'll drive you there!" She reached for her purse, as if we were going to walk out the door and drive to South Carolina right then.

"Mom, Columbia is an hour away. You can't drive me there. You can't leave Dad here for two hours."

"He's fine! He has the remote and a phone. He can get to the bathroom."

"He is going to be fine, but he's not so fine right now that we can leave him with no one home for two hours."

"He'll call a neighbor if he needs something!"

"Mom . . ."

"You are being irresponsible. This is stupid."

I was trying to be calm and mature and in control of the situation, and I had been fighting with an airline for two days, and my hair was dirty, and my kids wanted to know when I was coming home, and I loved Christmas, but I was missing Christmas with them, and my mom was yelling at me like I was a little kid, but I felt like *she* was being the little kid, and how could I have kids in both directions, older and younger than me? I didn't know how I was supposed to be the adult here. I shouldn't be leaving. I had to leave. How could I leave? How could I go if my mom thought it was okay to leave my dad alone in a recliner for two hours less than two weeks after open heart surgery? Who would be the one to think straight?

I'm not even sure *I* was thinking straight. Three adults in one house, and I don't know if we all added up to one fully functional mind.

"I have rented the car. I am going. *I have to go home.*" My voice broke. I lost it. The rest of the conversation was pretty much just the two of us yelling at each other as if yelling would cover up the fact that we were both crying. Imagine two hysterically quacking ducks:

Quack!
Quack!
Quack! Quack! Quack! Quack!
Quack! Quack! Quack!

I called a car to take me to the airport. My mom was not happy. I was not happy. I can only imagine my dad wanted to helicopter himself out of the house and into any other home on earth.

Before I drove home, I sat in the rental lot to get familiar with the car and give John an update on my plans. I didn't have enough of myself to go around. I didn't have enough time for everyone. I didn't have enough strength to resist crying. My parents needed me, and I was leaving. My mom yelled at me, and I yelled back, and what kind of person yells at their mom in that moment? What kind of asshole yells at a mother and a wife who has been awake for days on end, standing sentinel over her husband, guarding him from death?

I sat there blowing my nose in the car, waving politely at other renters walking past, and I thought, *There should be a place where people can do this.* How hard would it be to repurpose the old smoking lounges and designate a space where people can go to break down for whatever reason? A crying lounge could be stocked with cold beverages, soft chairs, windows to stare out of, large sunglasses in a range of sizes, fresh waterproof mascara, and friendly, quiet dogs of varying fluffiness. It could be centrally located but closed off, separate from the rest of the airport, just like time and space in the air are separate from time and space on the ground. Wouldn't it be lovely to have a place where we could privately fall to pieces and then get ourselves together? Instead, we have to do it out in the open.

When I got home, I slept. Back at my parents' house, Dad improved. Mom rested. Over time, the updates from my mother became shorter and less eventful. Dad went back to sleeping in a bed. Mom gave away the recliner. He returned to work for half days, then full days. Every passing month felt like a deeper breath. Winter passed, and spring dawned with a sense that maybe it had all been a bad dream. A bullet had whizzed by so close it nearly left a burn, yes, but it was just a close call. We all took to saying things like, "Aren't we glad that's over?" as if it really was. As if loss couldn't waltz right in and take anything it wanted, anytime.

THE OPPOSITE
OF A DAYDREAM

I had the first vivid dream of harm befalling one of my children when my daughter was about two.

Earlier that week, she and her brother had been roughhousing on the sofa, near a window, and they'd tumbled off the side. She had knocked into a nearby window so hard that she broke it with her head. She didn't fall out (and if she had, she'd have landed inches below, on soft ground); the broken glass didn't even cut her skin. She just hit the window and bounced back, landing her diapered bottom on the rug. From the next room, where moments earlier I had called, "Y'all quit wrestling on the sofa!" I heard the glass break and my son say, "Uh-oh."

"Mama, look!" he said when I came into the room. He pointed to the hole in the glass. "She fell out the window and then fell back in!" My daughter sat on the floor by the mess, as if she'd been lounging there all along.

A few nights later, as I slept, my memory replayed the crash, but differently. *What if . . . ?* my mind seemed to say. Here I was on this timeline, the one where she bounced back, but how close did we come to the other timeline, the one where a broken pane of glass slid into her neck? What made the difference in that split second? The angle of her gaze, looking back at her brother? The instinctive outreach of her arm to catch herself against the sill?

What if they had decided to play upstairs instead of downstairs that morning? What if she had fallen out my second-story bedroom window to the concrete driveway below?

I heard it, I was certain—it was as real as real can be—the sound of her head making impact, a wet, heavy *crack*. I took in a sharp breath as I opened my eyes and lifted my head from the pillow. Moonlight shone uninterrupted across my bedroom through the intact glass of the window. It was the middle of the night. Everyone was asleep.

I have had countless dreams like that one, brief sensations that last just a couple of seconds: the screech of tires, a voice calling, "Mom!" The dream scenes bubble back up for days afterward, piercing the membrane of reality with imagined sights and sounds. What do you call it when that happens while you're awake? Not daydreams; those are happy. What's the opposite of a daydream—a nightmare, but with your eyes open? A daymare?

Then there are the longer dreams, bizarre, extended sagas that play out for what feel like hours but are probably just a minute of sleep.

After a few waking hours, I lose the threads and the dreams dissolve, but here's a recent one I wrote down as soon as I woke up:

We are floating, the kids and I, in separate inner tubes along a gently moving river. There are other people swirling past on their own candy-colored plastic rafts. I have told the children to stay near me, but they keep drifting ahead, and I have to paddle awkwardly with my feet, my butt slung low in the hole of the inner tube, to catch up to them. My hands are full. For some reason, I am carrying a steel mixing bowl and two big, gray athletic shoes. I call out for them to pay attention, slow down.

Then I'm out of the water, in a locker room, changing clothes in a stall—or trying to, anyway. As I dig through a duffel bag, I find that all my things are covered in warm, soggy oatmeal. Blobs of it slide down the waxed canvas inner walls of the bag. I pull out a pair of jeans, but as I step into them and pull them over my hips, oatmeal oozes out of the pockets. I reach into the bag for a sweatshirt and feel mush.

I come out of the locker room and call for the children, but they don't come. I run out the front door of the building and stop when I see dozens more buildings: offices, hospitals, I don't know what they are. Are the kids in one of those?

My phone is in my hand. I touch my thumbprint to the "home" button, and shout, *"Call the kids."*

Nothing happens. I make myself slow down. "Call. The. Kids."

A man's voice comes out of the phone. He's an operator of some kind, breaking through on the line. "Ma'am, I'm sorry, but there has been an incident . . . a situation is unfolding . . . we are getting reports . . ." He is speaking in phrases that indicate breaking news, but he doesn't finish his sentences.

"What's happening?"

He doesn't answer. I am beginning to hyperventilate, because everyone knows you have to have a working phone in an emergency, and we never made a plan about where to meet or what to do if our phones didn't work.

That's when I wake up.

Are there people who don't fear for their loved ones at all? Or are there just some who speak their fear out loud and others who don't? Some who push the feeling down most of the time and others who act on it in ways that go beyond protective to problematic?

I know this: As children grow up, you can't stand in the way of all their comings and goings, blocking them from living their lives just because you fear harm will come to them. To let them grow and flourish, you have to pick your way carefully to the just-right level of caretaking. You can be concerned for their health and safety, because that's smart. You can even be fearful of danger, because that's natural, forgivable. But you have to decide where the line is, and you have to know that where you draw the line might not be where someone else draws it. We all know it would be going overboard to get up every day and tuck a child into one of those giant inflatable bubbles you can roll down a hill, but up to that point there's room for debate.

If you're deciding whether it's okay for your child to take a certain risk, whether they're allowed to do something their friends are doing, for instance, and you say, "I don't know, I'm afraid . . . ," you can be sure someone in your midst will judge you. You might insist you're actually pretty permissive. You always let them walk to the park by themselves when they were little! You don't even see them for weeks at a time in the summer! It's just that you can't get on board with this one thing, whatever it is—letting them drive on the highway at night when they've only had their license for a month, letting them go to a party on a lake with a keg and a boat and no parents. Still, someone will say, "Oh, it's *fine*. You're being paranoid. Let them go." You have to figure out how to care just enough but not too much, and then you have to ignore the people who call you a scaredy-cat. Let them be as brave as they wish with their own beloveds.

When I read articles scolding overprotective

parents or hear someone making fun of worriers—of women, of mothers, of fathers, of caretakers who express tenderness for others—I follow along, but I also think, *Hold up, buddy. How are you alive right now? Did you pop fully formed out of a petri dish and land on your feet in the street, with a head full of smarts and a nutritious meal in your pocket? Were you born knowing how to live? Did you raise yourself? Educate yourself? Hire yourself, pay yourself, give yourself the advice you needed to get started?*

Or did someone, somewhere, at least for a little while, worry about you, too?

A year after my son's epilepsy diagnosis, we were back at the children's hospital. He was there to be hooked up for an ambulatory EEG, the same kind of test he had in the hospital after his big seizure at home. We were trying to figure out if some small tremors he was having were anything to be concerned about or if he could safely ignore them. This time, the wires glued to his head would be connected to a portable, sandwich-size monitor, which would hang on a strap over his shoulder for twenty-four hours, measuring his brain activity while he went about a regular day.

It became clear on this visit that my son was physically outgrowing the children's hospital facilities. He was too long for the table, too tall for the chair. The neuro-diagnostic technician chuckled as she measured his melon head. He was Goldilocks and everything in this cabin was too small, but I still loved the place. Everyone was kind. Everyone was patient. Everyone moved slowly, carefully, showing their instruments before using them, explaining everything.

It is impossible not to feel grateful in a children's hospital if your child is alive. No matter what necessitated your visit, you can look in any direction and see something worse. Once, when we were there for my son to get an MRI— he was having awful headaches, possibly as a result of his medication, but we weren't sure— we had to wait over an hour past his appointment time because of an emergency. The radiology receptionist kept apologizing, and I kept insisting, "It's fine, no rush at all." There was a rush that day, of course, just not for us.

At our EEG visit, the walls of the room were decorated with decals featuring the characters from *Finding Nemo*, an animated movie my children watched dozens of times when they were small. I first saw it when it came out in theaters, just a couple of months after I gave birth to my son. I had no idea what I was walking into.

I thought it was a peppy movie about sea creatures, but no. If you've seen it, you know. As the movie starts, Marlin and Coral, a pair of clownfish, are admiring their pile of eggs and beginning to choose names for their babies when a hungry barracuda spots them. Marlin stops swimming. He stays very still and quietly begs Coral to freeze as well, but she cannot suppress her instinct to protect her offspring from the attacker. When she dashes over to her eggs, the barracuda sees her. It kills her and all but one of her babies. That's Nemo.

Please understand, I had exactly eight weeks of postpartum hormones surging through my body when I saw this scene.

"She . . . just . . . wanted . . . to . . . save . . . her . . . babies," I sobbed, clutching John's arm.

To this day, he teases me about my movie theater breakdown—how he whispered, "You're scaring all these children!" How I started giggling when I realized I was an adult making a scene at a kids' movie, but I couldn't help myself. How I knew I was being ridiculous even as I couldn't help being ridiculous.

Friends who are further ahead of me in life, who have already experienced some of the losses that pre-haunt me, swear that everything will be okay. They say, listen, the whole point of adolescence is to prepare for departure. That's why teenagers are so rebellious and messy and rude. The birds soil the nest, and then you're ready for the birds to go.

What if the birds don't soil the nest? Or they

do—and yes, it's maddening how they trash their surroundings as they bust out of their eggshells, how they snip and snipe and bristle at the affection they once welcomed, but not so much that you want to kick them out of it?

What if it feels like the world is stealing them from you, but you also know it is preposterous to say such a thing and that you can't even remotely behave as if you think the world is stealing your almost-adult children, because that's what an irrational person with a poor sense of perspective would say, and obviously you want your birds to learn to fly? What if you want them to go, because you want them to have full lives, but you also, simultaneously and secretly and impossibly, want them to stay by your side forever?

The things you can't say out loud find their way into dreams sometimes, where you can't be blamed for saying them, because you're asleep. That explains another dream I had recently:

There is no plot, not even a full scene—just a few seconds. In this one, I am screaming so hard I taste blood in my throat. I cannot see what I'm screaming at, but I feel it. It's a dark, hot suction in the air, like a fire backdraft. It's trying to pull everyone I love away from me.

It's some kind of vacuum hole, and I am enraged at it. It is not honoring the agreement I made with the universe. I promised I would take care of everyone I love, and I did; I took the best care. Now I am screaming, "THEY ARE MINE."

I am furious.

Then I am terrified.

I realize there never was an agreement.

I am shaking now, aware of how wrong I was.

I know, I know, I know: They are not mine. Everyone slips away. Everyone moves along. I'm not supposed to hold on to them. I shouldn't have said it.

When I wake up, my nails have made dark red crescents in my palms from how hard I was squeezing my fists. I swallow, and I am surprised my throat doesn't feel raw. But of course it doesn't. I was screaming only in my dream, because I know better than to utter them out loud, the words I must never, ever say: "GIVE THEM BACK."

PART FIVE

HOME AGAIN, HOME AGAIN

You're supposed to be careful what you wish for, but come on.

Just before the pandemic began, I made the decision to quit my bookstore job, so I could spend more time at home with the kids.

It was the period of time in which everyone assumed the virus hadn't arrived in the United States yet. Cities were shutting down in Asia and Europe. Italy begged the United States to prepare and avoid the fate of the Italian people. Here at home, the virus remained a strange news report from across the seas. Nothing had been canceled or even postponed. People seemed to think this would turn out like SARS or the swine flu—dangerous, even deadly, but nothing to panic about. (It turns out plenty of adults still assessed danger by the "Is this close or common?" scale I had used as a child.) At most, people were beginning to wonder whether they might have to alter their plans for conventions, conferences, and spring breaks in a couple of months. Meanwhile, everyone was still going to work, boarding planes, sitting in movie theaters. We were at the beginning of something, but we did not comprehend it yet.

At the moment, it was hitting me that my daughter would be starting high school in a few months and my son would be a senior. Increasingly, they were spending their time away from me, with classmates and friends and in the many activities that make up teenage lives. I could feel time moving faster, and I wanted to spend the minutes I could—the minutes they were willing to give me, anyway—with them, instead of sitting in front of a computer at night and on weekends in order to juggle my work and my writing. I wanted more of them while they were still living in my house. I wanted to make memories.

My daughter and I flew from Nashville to New York on a Friday morning at the end of February to celebrate her last middle school musical performance. For her combined Christmas-birthday-eighth-grade-graduation present, we had gotten tickets to see *Hadestown* on Broadway—a beautiful and strangely uplifting song and dance about death and love. By Sunday evening, we were back home, and by Monday afternoon, I had a dry sore throat. By lunchtime Tuesday, I had started feeling achy. By late Tuesday afternoon, I thought I had a horrible cold or had perhaps come down with the flu despite getting a flu shot.

John was traveling for work that week. In lieu of performing my malaise for his sympathetic audience in person, I texted him, hamming it up:

My lungs feel like fire. I have tiny razors in my chest.

Could I have inhaled aerosolized fiberglass or something?

Never come home. Save yourself. THIS IS THE HOUSE OF PESTILENCE.

Even as I typed, I chuckled. Drama queen.

Before I went to bed Tuesday night, I called him. "Do we have NyQuil? I can't find it." In my worst colds, it had always granted me a few hours of peaceful sleep. "Check under the bathroom sink," he said.

Swaddled in thick cotton socks, a pair of my dad's old blue cotton scrubs, and my oldest gray fleece college sweatshirt, I shuffled across the bathroom floor and squatted down to open the under-sink cabinet. Shaving cream, hydrogen peroxide, three bottles of conditioner, two large plastic cups . . . no NyQuil. I took a deep, jagged breath, coughed it out, and stood up. Downstairs, I rifled through every corner of the kitchen, pushing aside the coffeemaker, the knife stand, the dish soap. I found the box of green capsules, finally, lying on its side behind a pile of tea bags. My bones were burning. I was freezing. My skin hurt. I was shivering so hard the glass in my hand clattered against the metal tap as I filled it with water.

Wednesday morning, instead of waking the

kids right after my alarm went off, I went back downstairs to the scene of my frantic NyQuil search. I filled a stainless-steel salad bowl with warm water in the sink, added a few splashes of bleach, and dipped a rag into the pungent liquid. Then I wiped down every surface I had touched: the counter, the doorknobs, the handle of the refrigerator, the stair banister, everything. I opened the back door to air out the house. These were things my mom had done when my brother and I were sick, and that I had done a few times before when someone in our family brought home a nasty germ. I set out bowls of cereal, and stood across the room until it was time to drive them to school.

Throughout Wednesday, I lay on the sofa shivering, coughing. I scrolled through news on my phone, reading about how the first cases of the virus had arrived in the United States out in California, feeling glad we had made our trip to New York when we did. When I got bored and texted a friend—who had coincidentally been in New York at the same time we were—she confessed she felt like garbage, too. We joked about sharing the title of Tennessee Patient Zero. It was funny, because it couldn't possibly be true. Every official source said there was no chance the virus was here yet. We named our malady after the New York airport: LaGuardia-itis.

I had a magazine deadline coming up, but I was

too tired to craft sentences, so to give myself a project, I decided to plan a dinner party for when I felt better. I wanted to invite the young men who'd grown up in our house to come back and visit.

I live in the former home of a woman who raised her two children all the way to the brink of adulthood and then died. That's all I know about her. We bought the house from her husband, whose sons had grown up and moved out.

Since we moved in, each son has shown up at our front door, unannounced and unbeknownst to the other, to visit the house and ask to see their old room. One night about a year after we moved in, while I was finishing up some work at the kitchen table before dinner, the doorbell rang. I looked out and saw the shape of a man, and—completely unlike myself, because I don't open my door to strange men; I've seen movies—I walked right to the door and opened it. When he introduced himself, I said, "Yes, I know." The same thing happened four years later with the other brother. Each of them lingered on the back porch, in the playroom, by their mother's rosebushes. They looked just like the framed pictures that had been all over the house when we toured it, only taller.

When Jess, my real estate agent and friend, showed me the house the first time, she shook her head and said, "It's beautiful, but the energy is too sad." Jess could get away with comments about energy in a way that other people could not, because she'd had cancer in her thirties and treated it with both aggressive medical intervention and all sorts of spiritual healing practices. No one was going to say to her, *Cool it with the energy bullshit,* because for all they knew, the chants and incense were just as responsible as the chemo and radiation for keeping her alive. She took us to see several more houses, but I loved the first one. Even with its history, the house gave off a vibe of family and life. Plus, it was just the right size for us, surrounded by trees, and walking distance to a cattle pasture where we could visit cows and donkeys anytime. It felt right. So she helped us buy it.

Eighteen months later, Jess's cancer returned and she died, leaving behind her own husband and young son. A week before she passed away, when it was clear the end was near, more than a hundred friends gathered on her front lawn with candles at dusk and sang to her. She was too weak to come out, so she sat by her open bedroom window. Almost everyone outside had tears streaming down their faces, but other than the occasional sniffle, no one was noisily crying. I don't know about energy like she did, but if I were to try to describe it, I'd say it was sad, yes, because we were saying goodbye, but also almost tangibly positive. Together, everyone was contributing to a field of warm, yellow, pulsating love.

I have never thought this house has sad energy, but when I think back to how we came to live here, I always think about motherless children. I remember the man who built the house, who has since also died. I wonder whether, by the time he sold it to us, the house itself felt like a betrayal of the plan he drew up all those years ago to build a dream house for his bride. When we begin things, we can't possibly know how they will end. Everything we plan is built on guesses and hopes, never on certainty. It's a wonder anybody ever starts anything.

Spring would be coming soon, and the roses would be blooming. I imagined the boys—I thought of them as "boys" even though they were grown men—might like a chance to walk around and reminisce. I emailed them from my sofa and looked up lasagna recipes.

I repeated the bleach routine before getting the kids from school, feeding them something from the freezer for dinner, and sending them to bed early. I didn't want them around me while I coughed.

In twenty years of John's work travel, I had groused occasionally about feeling left alone to do the hard daily work of raising young children, but in the more recent years of our marriage, he had been the one often staying home while I traveled. I was proud of this partnership, the way we were able to preserve continuity at home by making sure the household always had at least one parent in it. I had never once asked him to cut a trip short, but at 4:30 in the morning on Thursday, I emailed him from my phone:

> *I think i am pretty sick. I am going to try to get to the walk.in clinic this morning. we might be approaching a point where I am not quite able to take care of kids So so sosorry . i think this is bad*

If you knew how much I love grammar and punctuation, you would understand why John changed his flight the minute he saw my note.

In the middle of the day on Thursday, I went to the health clinic in our pharmacy for a flu test. It came back negative within ten minutes. "Still, I'm giving you Tamiflu," the nurse said. "I'm looking at you, and I think you have the flu."

John came home and took over the bleaching and feeding. I retreated to the bedroom and told him to keep the windows open and stay away. He slept in the guest room. I rested, got four days of Tamiflu into my system, and thought I should be feeling better soon. He had another trip scheduled for the next week, and I told him to go. Surely, I was on the upswing.

By Monday at lunchtime, one week after I first started getting sick, I had started coughing the kind of thick, productive, metallic-tasting cough that feels like it's bringing up parts of your lungs that aren't supposed to be outside your body. I felt ridiculous for calling my doctor—I didn't want to bother her with a cold or the flu—but I made an appointment anyway. When I got to the parking lot, I turned off my car, rested my cheek on the steering wheel, and started coughing again. Every breath I tried to take turned into another cough. I couldn't breathe. I lifted my head and looked up at the medical building several yards away. *I'm going to collapse,* I thought, blinking tears.

A strep test and a second flu test both came back negative. My doctor prescribed a round of steroids, a stronger decongestant, and an albuterol inhaler—the same kind my daughter used. "Whatever you have, it's stubborn," my doctor said, as she sent me home.

The coughing wouldn't stop. I was hacking into a paper towel, which was coming back streaked with red. The back of my throat felt like it had something stuck in it. Trying not to panic, I texted my friend and fellow traveler. She, too, had quar-antined herself in a bedroom and felt so weak she hadn't been able to get out of bed in three days. "Do we have the virus?" we wondered. "We couldn't possibly," we assured each other. Both of us had been told by our doctors that it was out of the question, it wasn't in Tennessee yet. Both of us wanted to believe they were right. Both of us had seen the news that New York had confirmed its first case only the day before.

After I sent the kids to bed, I took a hit off the inhaler and lay down on my side on the sofa, positioning my face over the vaporizer, so I could inhale as much cool mist as possible between coughs.

An hour or so later, my son came downstairs to get a glass of water. He froze in the doorway of the den.

"Mom, are you okay?"

I didn't know what to do. I didn't want to worry him. He needed his sleep.

"Go back to bed, buddy. But for tonight, it's okay to take your phone into your room, just so you have it."

"I'll stay up all night, Mom," he said. "Then I can drive you to the hospital if you need it."

"No, no, no," I insisted. "You go to sleep. If I need your help, I'll call you and get you up, but I'll probably be fine."

That was as bad as it got.

Over the next several days, the coughing slowly subsided. The steroids gave me a burst of energy, which I funneled into maniacal housecleaning.

The boys were coming for dinner in a few weeks—we had to get ready! I pulled out a ladder and started scrubbing the kitchen top to bottom with a toothbrush. Why a toothbrush? I don't know! Did it have toothpaste on it? It may have! I might very well have detailed my baseboards with cool mint gel. I do know I called my sick friend and yelled, *"I'm Windexing the ceiling!"* because she still makes fun of me for it. I wanted the house to shine. I pulled all the old bottles of half-used dish soap and Lysol out from under the sink and rearranged them. I ran a rag around all the doorknobs. Then I took a six-hour nap.

A week later, the Tennessee governor announced the "first" case of the virus in our state—a man my age, one county over. Our dinner date with the boys had almost arrived, but we decided to postpone until it seemed safe to gather again.

Reports started coming out speculating that the virus had entered our country several weeks earlier than initially suspected, that it had saturated New York before anyone even realized it had arrived. My friend who had traveled the same weekend I had volunteered for a scientific study in which every volunteer was tested for antibodies. She tested positive. When I tried to volunteer, the study was full, so I asked my doctor whether it was worth testing me just for curiosity's sake. She said no, the labs were slammed. Plus, she added, no one was really sure whether knowing served any purpose anyway. Having the antibodies didn't guarantee immunity for any certain length of time, and she didn't want me to get a positive test, think I was safe, and then go run around town being reckless.

I laughed at that image: me, running around reckless, feeling free because of what I did not know.

Just as I was finally feeling better, everything started to shut down: school, sports, meetings, flights, conferences. Suddenly, there I was at home with the very people I'd quit my job to see more of, all of us together, every day.

In the mornings, I put breakfast on the kitchen table, placing plates of scrambled eggs on the same knotty pine slab that once supported piles of freshly folded baby laundry. Then, John, the kids, and I dispersed to corners of the house we claimed as work spaces: my home office, the laundry room John turned into a space for holding quiet conference calls with colleagues, and two "classrooms," one for each child to log into virtual classes and chat with classmates and teachers. We reconvened hours later, as if we had all just returned home from our normal daytime lives.

It wasn't exactly what I had in mind when I pictured "being home more." To be fair, I didn't quite know what to expect the first time I quit a job to stay home either. Seventeen years earlier, when I had stepped away from my full-time job at the American Cancer Society to take care of my son and write freelance for a few years, I wasn't taking some kind of principled stand. I've never believed it's better for parents to stay home. I just knew, in my gut, that my focus was shifting and I needed to follow that focus for a while. I wanted to be home, and I loved it—at least some of the time. What I hadn't anticipated was that the homebound repetition of feeding, washing, and napping would sometimes make me feel smothered, held captive.

I have a tendency, when I feel trapped, to feel a false sense of permanence. I don't think, *This is my life right now.* I think, *This is my life forever.* I panic. I forget, although I've learned it countless times, that every stage of life changes, then ends.

Back then, I dreamed of going to work in an office building again, wearing clean clothes. It burned me up when I took my kids to checkups and the nurses called me "Mom." *I'm not your mom,* I'd think. I'm not *everyone's* mom just because I'm *their* mom. As my years with children living in my house dwindled, I began changing my tune. Just before the pandemic began, I took my son and daughter to the dentist, and when the technician came out to the waiting room and said, "Mom?" I stood up and raised both hands. "Yes! That's me! *I am Mom.*"

If I could go back and tell my young-mom self one thing, I wouldn't whip out that cliché about how the days may pass slowly, but the years go by fast, even though it's true. I wouldn't say, *Just enjoy it!* I did enjoy mothering babies often enough, but also, some things aren't all that enjoyable. You don't have to feel joy while scraping mashed peas out of the cracks of a high chair. What I'd tell my young self is this: *Sometimes time moves quickly and sometimes it moves slowly, but it always moves forward. This is not your life forever.*

Back when my kids were babies, I couldn't have anticipated how much I'd love having teenagers. When I saw older kids skateboarding down the street, I used to think, *I'm so glad I have* these *and not* those. Adolescents seemed so big and loud. Who wouldn't prefer a sweet bundle of baby?

Let me tell you something, parents of babies. You know how that rush of affection for infants feels like a drug, how you sniff their heads and say things like, "I could eat you up"? Loving teenagers is not so much like taking drugs as it is a constant need to be sure that *they* are not taking drugs, and they don't like it when you sniff them, but listen: Loving a teenager is just as emotionally intoxicating as loving a baby. Maybe even more.

Plus, it's fun. Really. You can no more have a

conversation with your baby than you can have a conversation with a turnip. And sure, toddlers may say hilarious things like, "When I grow up, I want to be spaghetti." But my teenage daughter and I just had a long talk about how much we both love depressing movies, and it was amazing. You can't have Sad Movie Club with a baby.

I know plenty of people who don't feel this way. Lots of my friends and colleagues are in love with their jobs right now and wouldn't dream of stepping back. For many parents, cutting back on work while supporting a family is impossible; there are far tighter constraints than time. Too many employers still don't offer decent paid leave for the parents of newborns, so I'm not delusional enough to hope teen leave would take off. But wouldn't it be nice if it did? (We could call it ma*teen*ity leave. No? Okay.)

I used to think babyhood was the neediest stage of life, but teenagers need their parents just as much—maybe even more. A baby needs a snuggle, some eye contact, a song. A teenager needs a trusted adult to talk things out with when they or a friend gets into a scary situation. A baby needs clean, soft onesies. A teenager needs driving lessons. A baby needs to be fed at 1 a.m. A teenager who sneaks up the stairs at that hour needs to be greeted with a mix of love, relief, and stern clarity on the point that, no sir, you absolutely will *not* come traipsing in here that late again, and furthermore, where the hell have you been? Parental sleep deprivation comes in waves, apparently, about a decade and a half apart.

Maybe every aspect of parenting comes in waves. Every aspect of life.

If so, the kids and I were in overlapping waves, phases that had something in common. I might have just survived the virus, but they, like all teenagers, had just survived the car crash of puberty. We all looked like we were functioning normally, but our brains, theirs and mine, were in a state of continual change and occasional malfunction. We all needed a pause, some time to recover. It wasn't the worst time to be locked down at home.

As much as it felt like whiplash to go from wishing I could get a few more hours a week with my family to being holed up in the house together round the clock, I accepted that time greedily. I didn't tell myself I had to enjoy every minute, because I knew I wouldn't. Whenever the panic rose and we started to feel trapped, I reminded myself, just as I reminded them: This isn't forever. It never was.

SPATCHCOCK THIS

If I had a cooking show, it would be called, *What the Hell Am I Doing?*

In the pilot episode, a woman in her forties attempts to make Thanksgiving dinner for the first time ever, having somehow coasted along on the hospitality of others until now. She realizes that the bird she ordered in a burst of overconfidence from the organic farm, where the turkeys frolic contentedly in the sunshine among their feathered brethren until their one not-so-fun final day, is three times larger than she thought it would be.

Her plan is to spatchcock the bird. To that end, she has watched several videos demonstrating the "amateur-friendly" butterflying technique for faster, more even cooking. (You can ask the butcher to spatchcock the turkey for you if you get it from a grocer, but not if you've ordered it from the happy farm of endless sunshine. Then it's a do-it-yourself affair.) All she has to do is cut the bird's backbone out with a strong pair of kitchen shears and crack the front center bone; then the two sides of the turkey breast should fall open, like a book. When she tested the method on a chicken a few weeks prior to Thanksgiving, it took some muscle to break the breastbone, as well as some willful denial about the fact that she was breaking an animal's breastbone, but she did it. Although she herself has been eating less and less meat in recent years, she has failed to convince her family to have an all-potato holiday.

The problem is that this bird is bigger than the four-pound chicken. This is a twenty-three-pound beast, larger than either of the family dogs. It fit in the refrigerator only after two shelves were removed. Now, as our show follows along, our hostess is struggling to crack it open.

In a tragicomic scene, she has climbed on a step stool for leverage. With her hair piled into a bun atop her head and her bright green, turkey-gut-smeared cotton apron tied around her torso, she looms tall over the kitchen counter, where the enormous, round bird has taken up the full surface of the largest cookie sheet she owns, which rests upon a flattened plastic trash bag. She bends at the waist, leaning upon the slippery breast with both hands, doing chest compressions as if she is giving it CPR. "Staying alive . . . staying alive . . . *push push push push*." It doesn't crack.

She does not want to call her husband or one of her teenagers for help, even though they are all larger than her—she used to be one of the two biggest people in the house, and now she is the smallest—because she is determined to do this herself. She told them she could make

Thanksgiving dinner this year, because for the good of her parents and her husband's parents, they must stay away. They cannot risk spreading a virus during a pandemic. So by God, she has to learn to make this meal. She should have learned before now. A person of her age should know how to pull off a big holiday dinner from scratch.

It is one set of bones, skin, and meat versus another. They are both animals, but only one of them is alive. You'd think that would be enough of an advantage. The woman looks into the camera and ponders aloud what to do. "I'm going to need greater force," she says.

She wonders if she could take the turkey pan out to the garage and set it on the floor. She could put clean trash bags over both feet like boots, and then she could jump onto the bird from a ladder.

She is me, of course.

I embrace domesticity in fits, going all in, buying the supplies to undertake a project, and then, usually, finding out nothing is as simple as the instructions made it out to be. There is so much encouragement in recipes and directions, so much insisting that "anyone can do it!" The more accurate verbiage, which would create less false hope, might be, "Most people can do it after a couple of tries, but not everyone, which is fine, because some people have other talents!"

I used to half-joke that I didn't have an interest

in or talent for the domestic arts because that kind of thing skips a generation. But lately what I've been thinking, deep in the part of my brain with the other thoughts I don't want to put words to, is: *Someone needs to hurry up and learn how to do the things my mom has been doing all my life.*

In the end, I gave up on handling the turkey without help. I had to. I had managed to half-spatchcock it—the backbone finally removed after an awful lot of unseemly sawing and muttered apologies to the turkey—but, try as I might, no amount of pressure would make the center bone yield. At a certain point, it feels downright macabre to whale away at an already-dead bird. So I called John into the kitchen. When he saw the mess, he said, "Oh dear God," and laughed.

He rolled up his sleeves, washed his hands, and cracked the bird, easily. Then he took it outside to cook on the grill, because once it was spread out, it didn't fit in our oven.

The rest of the meal was fine, on average. The rolls were perfect, of course, because I bought them from a bakery. The gravy was vile, as was the second batch of gravy—both greasy, separated, oil-and-slime mixtures that, had I posted pictures of them online, would have gotten my accounts suspended for indecent content.

The cornbread dressing, a tradition at my mother's Thanksgiving table, didn't turn out quite as planned. On a video call, my mom walked me through how to make it. The important thing, she stressed, is that the cornbread must be completely dry, even a bit stale, which means you must make it three days in advance, which means . . . three days before this video call.

To make up for lost time, I baked the cornbread right away, while the turkey was on the grill. I immediately crumbled it into pieces and then put the pieces back in the oven to dry out some more. Then I forgot them. When I took the tray of crumbs out, they were brown. Toast. It was not right, but it was all I had, and it would have to do.

The scene that plays as the credits roll on my cooking show would be of my family at the table, John and the kids and me, chewing and smiling and laughing. You wouldn't be able to hear what we're saying, which is that the cornbread dressing isn't the same as my mother's, but it is reminiscent of hers. It *smells* like her dressing, at least, even if the texture is all wrong. Eating it is kind of like passing by a person on the street who looks like someone you once knew. Even though you know it isn't really them, you feel a sudden swell of joy at being reminded of them. I started too late, that was the problem, but at least I tried. And the potatoes were excellent.

INVESTMENT PIECES

I am always being told that something is an "investment piece." In the narrative pushed by certain fashion media, as well as the high-end stores I enjoy wandering into even though I sweat a little bit the whole time because I feel like I don't look fashionable enough to be there in the first place, shopping is not the whimsical acquisition of whatever looks cute on the rack in the moment. *Proper* shopping, as practiced by grown-ups with real money and real jobs and real lives, is the careful accrual, over time, of expensive items that will be folded in tissue paper, stored on cedar shelving in the off-season, and owned forever. And the height of investment fashion is cashmere.

A salesperson showing you clothing can't even say "cashmere" in their normal register. They have to drop it an octave or two. "Have you seen our line of classic crewnecks? They are one hundred percent [Darth Vader voice] *CASHMERE*." A cashmere sweater costs a whole paycheck, no matter what your paycheck amounts to, because, at least as I understand it, cashmere comes from the soft underbelly hairs of a goat that has been fed a frittata made of thousand-dollar bills for breakfast. Every respectable grown person needs a cashmere sweater in at least five colors. This rule was written somewhere, I don't know where, but I've often heard it repeated.

I am an easy mark. Shopkeepers can smell it on me, my longing to stop experimenting and settle into a capsule wardrobe that projects my core attributes to the world. They can sense, as they watch me thumb the edge of a cuff, that I've actually had this thought: One day, when a cartoonist draws me because I am someone who matters enough in the world to be rendered not only in photographs but also in colorful line art, I want the artist to know exactly what outfit to draw, because it's "so me." I give off this delusional desire.

They can tell that part of me wants to be the sleek CEO in monochrome suiting, and part of me wants to be the denim-and-black-separates cool girl, and a lot of me wants to be the cozy, be-scarved creative genius. They can even see that a small, reasonless part of me wants to be the character I see all the time on social media and in glossy pictures, the woman frolicking or lounging in the sun, with perfectly tousled hair, maybe on or near a boat, wearing a bikini and a wheat-colored, loose-knit, V-neck sweater. I am always entranced by this image. A bathing suit and a sweater? In what situation is your top half chilly enough that you need sleeves but your bottom half so warm that you don't even need pants? It can only make sense in a magical world where you can control the weather and conjure a different climate for each hemisphere of your body. If I were a witch, is that how I'd use my powers of sorcery? I don't know.

But I know I am very susceptible to imagery, and when a team of professionals engineer a picture or a retail display to subliminally tell me that I could be everything I'll never be if I'd just wear this or that particular garment, I often fall for it.

I answered the siren call of wool again and again, for a long time. Not just cashmere but other kinds, too. Merino. Angora. You name it.

Like many adults who used to be Southern children, I am acclimated to heat and hate to feel a chill. Plus, I run cold. Even in the summer, when I get into bed at night I stick myself to John like a magnet. Bless him, he only rarely curses out loud at the icy touch of my toes to his calves. I crave warmth, and wool promises it.

It also promises elegance. Behold the wool blazer—so classic! So polished! So hearty, sturdy, and time-honored. It's right there in the J.Crew catalog next to the cashmere scarves and something called an "Italian wool car coat." I don't understand why I would need a special coat to wear in a car, but I love the idea of wearing a sheep's hair, whether the sheep came from Italy or somewhere else. Sheep are real. I like sheep. I don't know what the hell a polyester is.

I have only just now accepted that wool makes me itch, always. If you, too, are sensitive to wool, you know that it can feel perfectly soft on the palm of your hand, but if left in contact with the more tender flesh at your neck or the inside of your elbow it sets off a miserable reaction within minutes. As soon as the itching starts, I heat up. Then I'm scratching *and* sweating. No one looks polished with bright red claw marks up and down their arms and purple splotches on their neck. For years, my closet was full of clothing that tortured me.

If an investment is something you put money into that then retains or gains value, then I need to face the fact that wool is not an investment for me, because its value is purely imaginary. It's a fantasy of protection and sturdiness and elegance.

I think I kept trying to wear wool for so long— just as I tried other activities that are supposedly good for me but actually make me feel bad, such as running and taking fish oil capsules—because I wanted to believe I had it in me to be a wool wearer. I wanted to believe that any version of myself I imagined could be true, if only I willed it.

In that way, wool is like a lot of things that

seem fun in theory but which, in reality, I do not like, such as staying up late. I love the late-night talk shows, and I get that they come on late because that's when everything is supposed to be loosened up and off the clock, but I cannot stay up to watch them. If I stay awake past midnight, the next morning my eyeballs feel shaky and my brain moves like sludge and everything everyone says irritates me, because all my body wants is to shut down and go to sleep. I want to think I could be a fun, night-owl, Peach Pit After Dark kind of gal, but being awake at 1 a.m. is my personal hell.

(John's the same way. In fact, he has been known to walk upstairs and go to sleep while a party is still going, both at our own home and in the homes of others.)

See also: rockslides, tequila shots, and riding in a convertible. I want to like things that look like fun, that other people do together to show how much they enjoy each other's company, that represent freedom and wildness. But tequila burns my throat. Rockslides hurt my tailbone. And have you ever tried to detangle your hair after even five minutes of speeding down the highway in a car with no lid? It hurts a lot.

Sometimes what the universe is telling me is not, *You can't have what you want,* but, *What you want does not exist for you.* There is no cozy wool sweater, not for me. There is no bright-eyed morning after a late night.

That means that if I'm being realistic, I have to give up not only those things I will never enjoy but also the state of wanting them. We all learn it sometime: A craving feels better, often, than getting the thing you crave. What a disappointment.

But maybe that giving up is also a kind of freedom. Wasting time scrolling online, trying to choose a soft-touch wool sweater that swears it won't itch, searching for the right long underwear to keep it from touching my skin—I don't have to do these things. I don't have to find a way to live with something I'm not required to live with. I don't have to buy into something that doesn't really have value to me.

There is one exception to my wool purge, a piece I haven't been able to get rid of.

It's a sweater I have owned for almost thirty years. I bought it because a boy I liked in one of my English classes had one just like it and he looked cute in it. It had personality, this sweater. In fact, this sweater probably had so much personality that it gave the wearer the illusion of a personality. It's possible I never did have a crush on the guy, just his sweater.

I don't remember how I managed to find out where he got it, but I did, and I went and bought the exact same sweater for myself. It was made in Scotland of wool that . . . I don't know wool-processing words, but I can tell you this wool was not . . . spun much? Or softened in any way? It feels like an actual sheep that has run through a field of thorns and brambles. It's almost impossible to fold, because it's so thick; all I can really do is kind of lump it in half and put it away. It takes up a drawer by itself. As such, it isn't particularly flattering. As rough and puffy as it is—cashmere it definitely isn't—it gives no hint at a human shape within. In it, I have no waist, no breasts. It comes down to my upper thighs, a wild and woolly brown bag.

I wore it often back then, when I thought it gave me something in common with a person I thought I liked. And then I forgot about the boy and forgot about the sweater for a decade. I got it back out one freakishly cold winter several years ago, when our heater had broken and I didn't know how else to insulate myself against the frigid air outside and inside our house. I wrestled it over two cotton turtlenecks, and it instantly and totally obliterated the cold. My bones stopped shaking. I breathed deeper. I relaxed and felt safe, not like a crazed animal seeking emergency hibernation.

Even now, when I've given away almost all the wool that was in my closet, I have kept this sweater. And not just kept it—continued to wear it. I put it on at least a few times every winter. It always works. If I wear something underneath that comes up to my chin and down to my fingers, if I make sure the sweater stays only on the outside of all my other clothes like a shell, it doesn't itch too much. I can barely move my arms in all the layers, but I don't feel the cold at all.

It has a stupid history, I look like a furry blob when I wear it, and if I'm not careful it gives me a rash—but I don't think I'll ever get rid of it. I make the rules, and I break the rules. So: no wool, except this one thing that does what nothing else can and that, if you look at it like an investment, has paid out dividends countless times over.

FACE HUNGER

The only way to get through this life without losing your mind is to make peace with the fact that you'll lose everything else at some point— maybe your mind, too—and there's nothing you can do about it. You can't hold on to anything, even your own face, which makes it awfully insulting that you have to look at it all the time. But maybe that's the job of our faces, to help us get used to letting go. Mine is giving me plenty of practice.

When I was in Wyoming to do a reading at a college a few years ago, my hosts took me out for a casual dinner. As we pulled open the heavy wood doors that led into the local watering hole, we were greeted by a wall-size bulletin board just inside, plastered with flyers for community events: rodeos, a blood drive, academic lectures, a demolition derby. And there, smack in the middle, was a poster for my appearance, complete with a huge version of my headshot. Suddenly and unexpectedly face-to-much-larger-face with myself, I nearly jumped backward through the wall. This is a great way to make a first impression, by the way, being a person who yells, "Ahh!" for no apparent reason upon entering a building.

I reflexively looked away from my own image, just like I do when I pick up my phone and accidentally tap the button that reverses the camera lens, confronting me with a close-range view of my nostrils—or when I walk into a hotel bathroom and catch a glimpse of myself at quadruple zoom. Who wants to see that much of their own face? Not me. That's why I always swore I would never, ever buy a magnifying mirror.

Then, after four decades of perfect vision, my sight evaporated. Friends had warned me that midlife brings farsightedness, but I didn't realize it could happen seemingly overnight. One day, I could read the tiniest text in any book just fine; the next, I couldn't decipher the ingredients in a recipe or the instructions on a pill bottle. For weeks, I tried to ignore the problem. I attempted to train my eyes to do more with less, adjusting my focus in and out like a kaleidoscope until my eyeballs ached; then I learned the hard way that the tube of zit cream and the travel-size tube of zesty mint toothpaste are the same size and shape. Lest I show up somewhere with eyeliner on my lips, I finally caved. I bought a pair of fuchsia-framed readers at the drugstore, and I installed a makeup mirror on a stainless-steel arm over my bathroom sink.

Oh. So that's what I look like.

I used to consider this bathroom accessory

the height of narcissism, a junkie's indulgence for selfie addicts hooked on micromanaging their complexion. Once I started spending a few minutes each morning and evening flossing and applying moisturizer in front of this round glass, however, I realized this felt nothing like taking a selfie. No one was watching, for one thing. I wasn't capturing the image and inviting a response. When I looked at my face up close, I was neither admiring nor judging myself. I was observing myself, in a sort of quiet, visual conversation. It was strangely intimate. Having not observed my countenance this closely in years, I was meeting it as if it were the face of a new friend.

Something about the arrangement of my features—the pointy chin, maybe the freckles—has always read as youthful. It used to be that with good light and some well-placed concealer, I could pass for a decade younger. Not anymore. Now my baby face has turned into my lady face. Since I last logged a mental image of it, everything seems to have shifted slightly downward, like a pie thrown at a wall, just after it makes impact and before it starts sliding. I notice broken capillaries, a spray of pink stars across my cheek. I did not detect the first silver strand sprouting from my crown, nor the second or third, but now I can see dozens springing from my head like electrified tinsel.

You can get a magnifying mirror at just about any strength: 3X, 5X, 10X, with or without a ring of light at the perimeter, wall mounted or freestanding. I went with 4X, no lights, enough to render my face as more than a pointillist portrait but not enough to illuminate the insides of my hair follicles. I wish I had bought it sooner. If I'd had it five years ago, I might not have succumbed on a whim to the poster advertising Botox in a dermatologist's office.

Before she would agree to do the shots, the doctor had asked, "Do you tend to emote with your face?"

Yes, I do, very much.

"No, I do not," I said. I didn't want her to withhold the injections that promised to make me appear fresh and relaxed.

For months afterward, I'd try to cock an eyebrow at something and all my poor toxified brow could do was lurch sideways toward my ear like a wounded caterpillar. If I'd been in better touch with my own face, I might have seen how when I raise my eyebrows high, my forehead folds up like an accordion. It looks funny—and it says whatever I'm making this expression about is funny, too. I would have seen all this *life* happening on my face. Perhaps I wouldn't have paralyzed it.

The Botox could not wear off soon enough. I never tried it again.

I did, however, begin to experiment with fancy skin-care potions. Some people keep their beauty products out on display, showing off the heavy glass bottles and pale, moonglowy ceramic jars. I keep mine in a cabinet under the sink. My secret showcase of gullibility includes an expensive serum that smells bad in a good way—like turmeric and something medicinal, but also roses, like a beautiful but stern nurse with soft hands and a big needle. I refuse to say out loud what I spent on it, but I would fight you like a dog if you tried to pry it from my hands.

I read a book once about how unnecessary and even harmful all this "self-care" is—how stripping our skin of essential lipid layers and then trying to put moisture back into it with creams and lotions is messing up our micro-biome. Intellectually, I understand this to be true. I know that I could probably save a bunch of steps and just stick with what I had in the first place: skin.

Is it vapid and misguided that my evening emollient ritual makes me feel cared for? Imagine if you walked into my bathroom and found me patting bad-smelling oil into my skin and said, "What are you doing?" and I said, "Caring." That would be a joke, right?

Well, joke's on me. Congratulations, skin-care companies—I'm hooked and in the boat. Now sell me some more of that sweet, sweet care.

• • •

Being middle-aged* means being between things—young and old, parent generation and child generation—and indeed, I am poised on the head of a pin. Half of me wants to figure out how to tighten up the crumbly edges and get my jawline back, and half of me wants to give up the burden of giving a damn what anyone thinks of my face.

Maybe that's why I came to love this mirror. Because what it reflects isn't for anyone else. It's for me. At work, online, in our interpersonal interactions, our selfhood is constantly being interpreted and consumed by others. You could easily slip into believing that what is reflected back at you by other people—you are a screwup, you are a star, you are important or irrelevant—is *you*. When you eliminate the middleman, when it's just you and the glass, all that goes away, at least for a moment.

---

*Although I can't stand the term *middle-aged,* I am learning to use it, because I understand that it efficiently conveys certain facts: I am more than halfway through the average American life span. I need certain medical care I didn't need before—hello, mammograms—but not the kind people need in their later years. I am not really of childbearing age, although I guess I could pull it off if I really tried; but I'm not of grandparent age by a long shot, unless something goes very differently than expected for one of my teenagers.

I just have to try to ignore the other connotations of "midlife": the end of relevance, the calcification of hairstyles, the acquisition of hokey dish towels and wall plaques about how both women and wine get better with age. If you ever hear me say, "They're not wrinkles—they're a map of my life!" hit me. They're wrinkles.

Middle age is such an awkward, self-conscious time. Maybe I hate the term because I hate being reminded of just how awkward and self-conscious *I am*. I'm still reckoning with the moment a few years ago when I saw a cute necklace in a store window and then looked up and saw that the shop was one of those chain stores that hawked neutral, waistless sacks and orthopedic shoes. I scuttled away like I'd accidentally looked into the eyes of Satan.

I swear the mirror taught me to look at faces differently. Not just my own but other people's, too.

For example, a new physical therapist entered my life during the pandemic. Having slacked off again on taking care of my back, I started meeting with Matt on a weekly basis in his airy, socially distanced, mask-mandatory clinic. While he applied hot wraps to my neck and guided me in doing exercises I ought to have been doing at home already, we chatted about his life. I knew

Matt had a new baby at home, an infant sister to his toddler daughter, a spunky girl with red hair like her dad's. Everyone at his house was tired, but they were hanging in there. I could have told you all sorts of things about Matt—that he loved watching football, that his grandfather was an accomplished cellist, that he favored a particular brand of quasi-athletic cushioned loafers—but I could not have picked his face out of a lineup. If he'd had to identify me from a photo, he probably couldn't have done it either. Matt and I formed a whole relationship, a cordial, ongoing acquaintance, without ever seeing each other's entire faces.

When we were all masked, I got used to seeing only the slice of face between a person's hairline and the bridge of their nose, but I missed seeing people's faces. Their *whole* faces. I missed seeing mouths twisted sideways in indecision, teeth bared in silly grins, upper lips curled in confusion, pouting lower lips, wrinkled noses, clenched jaws, all of it.

At a time when we had lost the comfort of physical proximity to others, the mirror also served as a kind of crutch. There was something oddly comforting about at least being able to get close to myself. Skin hunger—the sense of physical and emotional malaise that comes from a lack of being touched—is a known phenomenon, one that became newly familiar to quarantining people all over the world. But what about face hunger?

English has a word for something similar: *Pareidolia* means seeing familiar shapes in unfamiliar objects, including seeing faces where none exist. That's what happens when you look at a cloud and see a cherub-cheeked smile, or when you spy Jesus in your toast. It's why I imagine my car's front grille and headlights are grinning at me. Our brains are wired to detect faces. They interpret lines, curves, and shadows as faces so often because they're constantly scanning for meaning, and faces mean a lot to us humans.

It feels good to see and be seen in return— always, but especially when separated from the rest of humanity. We need to lay eyes on one another just like we need to lay hands on one another. Being unable to do so creates a particular kind of yearning, even grief. Say what you will about the ending of *Cast Away*; to me, the saddest scene in the movie comes when Wilson the volleyball floats away, leaving Tom Hanks sobbing for his friend with the face made from a handprint.

I have had a scar on one eye ever since I had surgery for a benign cyst right after I was born, but for most of my life I had not been able to remember where it was, because I didn't look at my own eyes. When people noticed it, they'd say, "What happened there?" and I'd point at my left eye and then my right. "Here? Here?"

Now I knew exactly where that identifying mark was, because twice a day I saw its faint apricot color nudging against the dark blue iris of my right eye. I would never have figured it out without my mirror.

The mirror reminded me that I was a person in the same way everyone else was a person, which is an odd thing to say, but maybe you know what I mean. Sometimes I felt like everyone else was a real-live, walking and talking human and I was just part of the background, an omniscient narrator of the illusion I saw as the world. Everyone else was an active object, but I was the wall. I was the atmosphere. I forgot that I had this face—these eyes, this nose, this mouth. I was no more and no less a body than everyone else.

Sometimes as I looked into my new mirror, I thought about what the poet and novelist Ocean Vuong wrote in *On Earth We're Briefly Gorgeous*, that the human eye is "god's loneliest creation." This line, in particular, stuck with me:

> *The eye, alone in its socket, doesn't even know there's another one, just like it, an inch away.*

It made me happy, thinking I was giving my eyes the gift of seeing each other. *Here you go, eyes. Don't be lonely anymore.*

• • •

I didn't time my blurry near-field vision to coincide with pandemic-era face deprivation. It just happened that way. But my longing for faces made me greet my own with extra interest and kindness. When I looked at a friend or store clerk from a safe six-foot distance—the distance at which, conveniently, I could still see without glasses—that longing made me zero in on what masks didn't cover: the color of eyelashes, the curve of earlobes. I could see details, pores, tiny pulsing movements, telegraphing the truth that we are each so strong, so delicate, so singular.

You can see it if you really look: We are all so alive.

IN MEMORY OF TURTLES LOST

My daughter opened the front door after a walk with a friend and called out, "Mom, I need to tell you something you really won't like." *Oh no,* I thought. Did a stranger in a trench coat flash them? Did someone in a van pull over and offer them drugs? Many of my catastrophic imaginings still come from those after-school specials.

"Over there." She pointed up the hill of our driveway, toward the curve of the road. "I didn't want to look, but . . ." Dammit, it was a flasher, wasn't it? "The shell is broken, and the body is definitely dead."

"Oh! Sweetie, I'm so sorry. Is it . . . ?"

"I don't know if it's him, Mom." Her chin trembled.

"Would you like me to come look with you?"

"Yeah," she sniffled.

We trudged up the driveway, both of us hoping out loud that the hit-and-run victim she had seen on the street wasn't Frank. By now, Frank had become almost as much a part of the family as our dogs, although unlike the dogs, Frank was not a pet. While we offered him an occasional snack of parsley and tomatoes, we mostly left him to eat according to his diet of foraged plants and various creepy-crawly proteins. He still came and went as he pleased.

Over the past several months, the pandemic had warped everything that had once been predictable about life for our family. Our home had turned into an office, a schoolhouse, and a poor replacement for our favorite restaurants. Our existence had transformed from a complex machine with many moving wheels and cogs to a sealed-off container. Four people in one house, all day. I loved the closeness, but periodically the reason for it washed over me like an icy tide: We're enjoying all this time together because we're hiding from a deadly virus blazing through our species.

I worried about my friends who were getting sick and my friends who were isolating, trying to stay healthy. I worried about my parents, my father still going to work and possibly being exposed to the virus every day in a hospital, and my social butterfly mother feeling lonely at home. I worried every time I got another notice—more and more of these emails every week—that someone's parent or brother or colleague had passed away. A dear friend and neighbor my age died, and I worried about the family she left behind. All funerals were "to be held at a later date," and I worried about what that wave of deferred mourning would do to all of us. I worried about my friends who were small-business owners, doing the discouraging math on how much longer they could stay closed until they could no longer afford rent. I worried about my children for all the same old reasons right alongside these new reasons.

And yes, by summer, I even worried about Frank. Every warm day that we didn't see his leathery face, I wondered if something had happened to him. A hawk, a lawn mower, an illness? It's normal for him to disappear from our lives for weeks at a time, but tell that to a mind that has gone into a full worry spiral.

One Saturday morning, we humans had been sitting on our back porch, contemplating what to bake next, when I heard a rustle behind me. I turned to see Frank shuffling through the grass.

"Frank!" I yelled. We all jumped up and ran to encircle our beloved reptile, exclaiming, "We missed you!" and, "You're back!" with the kind of weepy relief that must have made our neighbors think we'd just welcomed a brother home from war. We sat down on the ground and let Frank toodle around us. I am never less than thrilled to see him. It feels like pure wonder and delight, like I'm being visited by a deity or a tiny, time-traveling dinosaur. Someone brought out an apple slice.

• • •

John and I had been talking a lot in those days about what we would do in a few years when our nest emptied, whether we'd stay in this house or downsize and move somewhere else. Would we really want all this space, for just two people?

I never thought I'd consider the subject without heart-stopping despair, but lately, in glimmers, I was starting to think of the decades ahead as a pleasant reward. It was a relief to realize that I did not feel only loss when I pictured life after the children's leaving. I also pictured a chance for John and me to relax and rediscover things we love about each other and ourselves. He thinks this will include my taking up golf. Mark my words: It will not. Still, we'll have fun, I think.

One of my favorite things to imagine, when daydreaming about our future, has been our retirement house. *Retirement* is the wrong word, I admit; I'll never retire. That's part of what makes this a fun hypothetical exercise, thinking up the home-office-writer's-retreat of my dreams. It could have bookshelves with a ladder. It could have room for a reading sofa next to the desk. It could be anywhere.

I have always liked this part of the country— the Mid-South, people call it—but I don't know if I want to stay in the Nashville area for the long term. In our next phase, we might like to live farther out, in the country, maybe even build a house from scratch or fix up an old structure. Why not keep an open mind, at least?

When I started researching places to live, I thought perhaps I should consult some climate prediction data before picking a spot. Having woken up countless times to news of wildfires in California and hurricanes along the Eastern and Gulf coasts, I didn't want to invest time and money establishing a home in a place that might not be inhabitable after a few decades.

I intended to do some harmless googling about topography, but before long I had fallen deep down a climate change rabbit hole. I pulled up a set of maps one day showing projections for the next fifty years based on fossil fuel consumption and carbon dioxide emissions. As temperatures continue to rise and weather becomes more erratic, the frequency of fires and floods will go up, the maps clearly indicated. I looked at where my parents lived: I understood that they wouldn't be here in fifty years—nor would I, for that matter—but I was still alarmed to see that their town in Georgia fell into an area marked in red, a region where it will become difficult for human bodies to cool themselves during some parts of the year.

I wondered whether doing construction or renovation would be an irresponsible choice, given the state of things. I looked up green building standards. I became obsessed with solar power.

One afternoon I spent ninety minutes watching a presentation online about collecting rainwater. Rain barrels are for hobbyists, the lady in the video said. You need something much bigger if you want to reuse collected rainwater for irrigation and toilet flushing. John walked into the kitchen that evening, and I greeted him with, "What do you know about cisterns?"

I read about cove forests, riverbeds, and various types of ground cover. I learned more about trees, just as so many of us are learning more about plants and animals and water now that we've collectively realized that humans have spent the earth's resources with a false sense of endless abundance. The more I knew, the more I noticed. I found out, for example, that rhododendrons, which I had always associated with cool Appalachian mountain air, are not fire-resistant at all. They're like having a huge box of matches planted right up against your front door. Yikes.

For months I dug deeper into my dual obsessions: dismal climate research and the house I was building in my mind. Home dreaming and doom reading became my conjoined hobbies. I downloaded a United Nations report predicting the world will become "an uninhabitable hell" if countries don't cooperate in taking big, drastic actions. I looked up induction cooktops. I read an article weighing the pros and cons of using lumber in renovating old homes; then I started mapping out the floor plan for a guest suite. (My imaginary house plan had long since gone past anything we could ever afford into pure fantasy territory.) I could invite all my friends to come visit, and maybe we'd have a sign-up calendar where they could pick their weekends and it would always be full. I could learn to compost. Could my own body be composted one day?

Scenes of horror and scenes of joy flickered across my mind seconds apart, like I was clicking back and forth between two very different TV stations. The problem with imagination is the same thing that makes it great—it can go in any direction, even two directions at once.

At the height of this fixation I asked a real estate agent to show us some land. That sounds grand—"some land"—but really it was just a little wooded hillside, half an hour from the nearest town in one direction and half an hour from an airport in the other. I had begun making a budget and a timeline for replacing my gas-powered car for an electric one. Everything we would need was in range of a good battery charge. I did not mention to the agent that we were not even remotely prepared to make such a purchase; I just wanted to see it. I wanted to stand, for real, in the kind of place I was imagining and think, *Could we live here?*

The agent who showed us the property had grown up in the area. As we tromped through high grass, I asked, "So, you must get a lot of animals around here?"

"Oh yes," the agent said. "Lots of deer. Turkeys. Bears, supposedly, although I've never seen one myself."

"Turtles?" I said, sounding casual, I thought. I heard John chuckle behind me.

"Haven't seen those," the agent said.

"Well, they can be hard to see," I said. He nodded.

We stopped and took in the view: trees, a distant clearing, gray-green layers of mountains far in the distance. I still couldn't decide whether I wanted to live in the middle of nowhere or near other people. Sometimes I thought the latter— neighbors look out for one another, and close social bonds supposedly prolong life. Then again, sometimes I just want to be left alone, plus it's not like I'm great at socializing with the neighbors I have now.

It occurred to me that if we left, we would have to say goodbye to Frank. Box turtles stay in their home territory all their lives. It's cruel to remove them to another area, because they will wander forever after, attempting to get back to the place they know.

"If we ever move," I said when we got back from looking at the land, "I think I'll make an orientation booklet about Frank for the new owners of this house." I began thinking about what I would include: pictures identifying Frank's companions, notes about which shrubs they like to burrow under, a plea not to use insecticide or herbicide in the yard—

"Well, remember," John said, interrupting my planning of the turtle's biography, "we don't know how old Frank is. He may say goodbye to us before then."

I hadn't thought about that.

My daughter and I rounded the curve from the driveway into the street. I had wondered often over the past two years whether I was damaging her somehow, neglecting her needs whenever I tended to her brother's. But this girl was okay—full of joy, so curious about the world around her, so *herself*. Maybe fretting over my split attention had been a waste of my time, a needless drain on my own energy.

She stopped, and I proceeded in the direction where she pointed. There it was, at the muddy edge of the black asphalt. An intricately whorled dome, cracked into pieces and smashed over a mottled leg, a four-toed foot, a gray head flattened, one lifeless amber eye still open. My heart broke. If I could step in front of the car that did this and scream *Stop!* I would, but it happened when I wasn't looking. I couldn't fix it.

I've come to recognize our little friend's size, color, and distinct shell pattern, so I knew instantly: This wasn't Frank. Nor was it any of the three other repeat turtle visitors we can identify (Shirl, Taco, and Louise, all named by the kids—we never did determine whether we had seen Fancy again, or if Fancy had ever been a separate turtle from Frank in the first place). "It's not one of ours," I called to my daughter. *But it's someone's,* I thought. Everybody comes from somebody.

There is a difference between grateful and glad. I was grateful that this wasn't Frank, but I wasn't glad any turtle had been hit.

As we made our way back down the driveway under the shade of the ash trees, we debated what to do. If it were Frank, we probably would have held some sort of funeral. We might have thought about burying him, although that would make no sense. We live on the ridge of a wooded hill, where coyotes roam and big birds fly overhead. A fresh turtle would make a satisfying meal for an animal or two. It wouldn't be fair to hide all that food, although nothing about this situation seemed fair. Every creature is made to withstand some forces and break under others. The line between the two is what defines one's place in the brutal, bittersweet natural order, but nature's design could not have protected this creature in such an unequal battle. When it's truck tires versus turtle, tires always win. We decided to leave the poor thing where it lay.

My daughter and I lingered by the front door. We discussed how if you're going to operate something as heavy as a car, you have to be very careful of others, although even a good driver might not see a turtle. We talked about how near misses remind us that they won't always miss, how no one can hide from bad news forever, and how lucky any of us are to wake up and live another day. I heard myself making a lesson out of it—making it seem as if the turtles lived and died to teach us about loss and tragedy and hope and optimism—and I allowed us this small story.

As I went inside and my daughter went back outside, we agreed we would welcome Frank even more joyfully next time we saw him, knowing that the worst worries do come true, sometimes, but not always.

I WOULD LIKE TO REPORT AN ATTACK UPON MY SOUL

My child's pediatrician has just handed me a brochure titled *Getting Your Baby Ready to Leave Home*, and I was fully unprepared for such an assault on my spirit today.

I thought he was going to hand me the slip of paper that shows my child's height and weight, which I realize is a less relevant piece of information as my child approaches six feet tall and *my child* becomes less of an apt term, size-wise and age-wise and possessive pronoun–wise, what with my baby being 216 months old.

I thought we were going to talk about the latest adjustment to his medicine, how he has been having headaches and has lost some weight, which is not great, but the good news is that this latest anti-seizure medication is working. He has had only the tiniest tremblings, no major seizures in two years, which is quite a run.

I knew I would not be handed some kind of official receipt showing that after two years of research and worry and love and pill slicing I had learned all the important lessons about how nothing is really within my control and we all have to be flexible and life is full of surprises. It's not like I actually thought we would talk about the fact that *I did it.* I loved him hard enough, and we treated him well enough, and we figured it out, and we held on to him. We did not let the surges of electricity in his brain take him. We kept him here.

I didn't *really* think a nurse would come in and say, "Good job, Mom. The epilepsy can be over now." I know it isn't. But I didn't think we were going to talk about other sorts of ending either. I thought this was just a checkup. I thought we might each get a lollipop on our way out of this office. I did not come in here expecting to be handed a machete and told to cut the cord. Is that something they teach doctors in medical school?

Sure, when I think ahead, I do think about what it will be like to wake up every morning to one big, malleable stretch of daytime and not three to five segments of hours or minutes between requisite mealtimes, schooltimes, and bedtimes. I do occasionally look at my kitchen table and imagine what the surface of it looks like, a surface I have not seen in nearly two decades, covered as it has been in dishes, pencils, papers, and keys. I do think about how much fun it will be whenever a grown child comes home to visit—how every time will feel like a celebration. I may or may not have planned some of those menus already. I do anticipate my heart overflowing with pride when I see that a child who once couldn't figure out how to operate a spoon has successfully learned to manage a budget and maintain an apartment. It will feel so good.

But I was going to ease into all that.

Childhood is full of beginnings. Every fall when we're young, we get to start over in a new grade, as if our lives are getting a routine software upgrade. New notebooks, new erasers, different lunch table, different person. Without that automatic opportunity to reintroduce ourselves to the world, adults get a chance at a reboot only if we manufacture it. A few years ago I started looking at each fall as if I'm starting the next level in school. In fortieth grade, I set my alarm clock ten minutes earlier to make my mornings more peaceful. In forty-first grade, I remodeled my office. I've made myself a reading list for forty-second grade, because I want to enter forty-third grade with a broader perspective on the world.

It's goofy, I guess, to think of myself as a still-growing child, but it's also thrilling to remember that although it has been my job for so many years to help my children grow up, I am still growing up, too. I am becoming someone, still and always. I enjoy setting my own timing for a reset every year. It helps me look at life less like one ending after another and more like a series of starts.

So forgive me if I am shaken by this rather abrupt announcement of a finish line. It's not that I haven't been thinking about it all this time. I just didn't know this was the day I'd get the brochure in my hand.

My boy is alive. My boy is okay. He is only taking a step away from me. The thing is, one step leads to another leads to another leads to the last, for everyone, and—because the mind has no guardrails—it's hard to think about some endings without thinking of others.

I still read sad books, so I have, in recent years, beheld some beautiful new thinking and writing about death. Doctors who see it up close, in particular, have articulated the end of life as we know it in ways that are, if not reassuring, at least less grim. People with terminal illnesses who also happen to be tremendous writers have memorably articulated their final months. Your consciousness lives on in the memories housed by your loved ones' consciousnesses, they suggest. Your atoms return to Earth's atoms. There is a holiness or, for the less devout, a wondrousness in the way the cells of the body transform in the process of death. It is amazing, scientifically speaking. It can be, for some, a peaceful end to suffering. It can be something for loved ones to be present for, to look directly at and even participate in, versus something to turn away from. We must live with the reality of death, goes this thinking, not fight in vain to deny it.

I appreciate this thinking so much. I will get there. I am not there yet.

I also don't know that all this eloquent and evolved thinking about death makes up for death itself. Show me a person who has lost their most loved human being—their mother or spouse or daughter or brother—and I'll show you someone who would trade anything, *anything,* to get those atoms out of the earth and put them back together as their dear one.

Life can't be all beginnings, but I am still a little stuck on the fact that I don't want my people to go. I'm a little stuck on the idea that what I want has anything to do with anything.

When they are here, right in front of me, I can see and touch their long, lean limbs and feel in my hands their bendy, chubby baby arms. When they are not here, I know they're out there, but I miss them. And I also miss what became one of my life's great purposes, caring for them. I had other purposes before they were born, and I have other purposes still. But that one purpose rose out of the water like a volcanic mountain and eclipsed the rest. It is hard for a human being not to have a purpose or, at least, not to have the one that for so long dominated all the others.

It is not intellectually fashionable to rage against the dying of the light, but here I am, and here is this brochure about my child leaving.

"You have raised a wonderful child," the brochure begins. Thank you for noticing, but also, what is with "have raised"? That phrasing is violence upon my emotions. Blunt-force psychological trauma.

I can't get my verb tenses right. This person, my son, is going to leave my home and sleep somewhere else and have a whole life away from me, I know that, but right now I am looking at him and thinking, *He is my child,* and you're telling me that's about to be over? I don't understand how parenting will become *past* if I always love my children in the *present*.

I just got here. And by *here,* I mean here in this exam room and also here on this earth. My child just got here. We are just figuring this out. What is this "leave home" situation? *I am* my child's home. Just ask my uterus.

What's that? My uterus is not picking up the phone?

Fine.

The point is: "Home" is the state of warmth and safety and love among the inhabitants of my heart, so *leave home* does not make sense.

The words splashed across the back of the brochure cheer, "You're doing great!"—but I'm not so sure. I did not know I would be told today that it's time to have my child ready for adult life. I barely feel ready for it myself.

ANOTHER BOX,
ANOTHER CHRISTMAS

A couple of years ago I signed up for the Nextdoor app, thinking, *This will be useful when we need a plumber.* I must not have realized at the time that I would be getting emails daily, anytime a fellow Nextdoor user from my general part of town posted an update. I certainly did not know that Nextdoor subscribers, at least in my region, use the app primarily to quarrel about outdoor decor, self-report scams they have fallen for, and speculate as to the identity of animals they have seen in their yards.

It's that last category that keeps me from unsubscribing. I cannot get enough of the "Is this a coyote?" emails, especially the ones that don't have a picture attached. *Did* you see a coyote today, Marjorie? We can only guess. Last week, I got four emails about lost cats, two of which were resolved with follow-up posts announcing the cats were home all along, hiding in pantries or closets, never missing at all. I am hooked on this low-stakes entertainment.

One evening, just after I finished reading a post about an armadillo sighting, I came across a note that began, "My name is Ava, and I am a college student." I had never seen a Nextdoor post from someone so young before. In fact, I had come to assume that I was a few decades younger than the average Nextdoor users.

I clicked to read the email. Ava, a senior at one of our local universities, wrote that because of the raging pandemic, she could not go back to her hometown during winter break. Her parents were caring for her elderly grandparents, and she and her family had decided that it was safer for everyone for her to stay in Tennessee. She asked whether anyone could recommend a soup kitchen or other charitable organization that might be open on Christmas. She wanted to spend the day helping others to take her mind off the fact that she was alone in her campus apartment, away from her family.

I held my phone out to John and said, "Read this."

It was December, two years after the night I lay on the floor staring at the ceiling. College students were already on my mind, well before I saw what Ava wrote. Here at home, I had been saying yes to everything—yes to watching another Christmas movie, yes to cake for breakfast— because I wanted to soak up every second of this season together. Our son had recently gotten into college. We had started preparing him for life outside our house: teaching him to cook his favorite foods, making sure he knew how to check a car engine. He had begun cleaning out his room, giving books he no longer wanted to his sister, tucking his special stuffed animal from toddlerhood into a safe drawer of his desk. I had taken to slipping into his room when he wasn't in it, standing for a few seconds and inhaling the smell of his occupancy: sweat, shoes, Old Spice, shampoo.

Life might have taught me not to count on anything for certain, but the way things were looking, the next time Christmas rolled around we would most likely be waiting for our boy to come home from college on a break. He wouldn't just *be* here, like we were all here now; he'd be paying us a visit. Hauling a laundry bag. Partially unpacking before leaving again.

I had just been picturing this scene when I saw Ava's post. After John read it, he handed me the phone and laughed.

"I know what you're going to do," he said. Of course he did.

All my friends with older kids had said that the beginning of college wasn't the end of parenting, that the kids come right home for a while every few months. That was the deal: You could move on and plan fun things, because *they'll be back.* But here was a girl just a couple of years older than my children, away at college, and she couldn't go home. Her parents would be having Christmas without her, and she without them.

"This must sound bizarre coming from a total stranger," I typed, "but I would be so happy to put together an extra plate of Christmas dinner for you. I'm cooking anyway, and it would be zero trouble. We could deliver it to you at school, or you're welcome to come pick it up from our house." If this girl was going to spend her lonely Christmas feeding others, the least I could do was feed her.

Ava wrote back to say she would love to take us up on dinner and that she and her boyfriend—also stranded on campus at another nearby university—had decided to wait out the holidays together. If we didn't mind feeding them both, they would be thrilled to come say hello and pick up dinner on Christmas afternoon.

I was so happy. This is what I would want someone to do for my kids, if they found themselves stuck away from home at Christmas. I would want someone to mother them for me.

I have been mothered by stand-ins more times than I can count. By professors who had me over for dinner in college. By strangers in airports who tapped me on the shoulder to hand me a dropped boarding pass. Even by people I've never met in person.

In the early heyday of the Food Network—when it aired mostly instructional cooking programs, not game shows and extreme-dining exhibitions—John and I were young newlyweds and he traveled often for work. Most weeknights, I came home from my office and watched a show called *Cooking Live*, hosted by Sara Moulton. Because each hourlong episode was broadcast live, Moulton had to roll with mistakes as she made them. If she spilled oil on the stove, she gave a demonstration of how to put out a grease fire. If she burned a pie crust, she turned the show into a talk about how to salvage the rest of the dish when one element gets ruined.

She said, "Remember, salt your pasta water," and I heard: *You are not alone. You can make a real dinner that isn't a bowl of boxed macaroni. Some parts of adult life are hard, but not all.*

I learned knife skills and how to season meatballs, but the most lasting lesson Chef Moulton taught me as she chatted amiably into the camera was that it is possible to make someone feel cared for from afar. Even now, I think she's why I sometimes imagine I'm hosting a cooking show in my own kitchen.

On the night of September 11, 2001, when John was stuck at a meeting in Texas and could not get home, I sat alone in our house. I wanted comfort, so I turned on the Food Network, but Sara Moulton wasn't there. Instead, an on-screen message announced that programming had been suspended due to the day's events. It was the right thing to do—how could anyone have hosted a cooking show that night?—but I wonder if anyone at the network realized what they had taken away from people like me, who watched their shows because it felt like being taken care of, who were not children anymore but still needed auxiliary mothering.

I want to believe that if humans really leaned into this impulse to mother one another, it would be stronger than the impulse to tear one another apart.

Early Christmas morning, a bomb went off in downtown Nashville.

The alerts were blinking on our phone screens when we woke up; it had already happened. It was the kind of news you have to say out loud a few times before you believe it. "A *real* bomb? Downtown . . . *today?*" Apparently, it was too early to know anything about the bomber's motive, although there was speculation that the person responsible for wiring the RV to explode had been in it at the time and died in the blast, so there was also a sense that motive might remain a mystery.

John and I sat in bed and clicked on various news links. People who lived in nearby apartments overlooking what was normally a busy commercial and entertainment district street—but which was quiet on Christmas morning—reported hearing a message of warning over a loudspeaker. We opened a video someone had posted, which showed a large camper parked by a curb. You could clearly hear a recording repeating in a creepy, robotic voice, "This vehicle has a bomb. If you can hear this message, you need to evacuate."

We had internet, so we could send texts, but we couldn't make calls, because the bomb had taken out an AT&T switch center. Every half hour or so that morning, I slipped my phone from my bathrobe pocket to check for updates: Open a few presents / check on the bomb news / get the cinnamon rolls out of the oven / look at the latest headlines / text family members to say Merry Christmas / refresh the news feed. I wondered if there might be calls for volunteer assistance of some kind. Did anyone need food, clothes, help cleaning up? Police urged people to stay out of the area. A whole chunk of downtown had been reduced to rubble, but everyone within explosion range had gotten out safely. No additional casualties were reported.

I thought about Ava and her boyfriend, who were coming over that afternoon to pick up dinner. Imagine waking up on Christmas, at school, without your family, when you're still barely more than a kid. Imagine waking up on Christmas, at school, without your family, to discover your city has been bombed.

I went overboard cooking. No turkey this time,

but a feast of butternut squash ravioli with ricotta, stuffed potatoes, salad, fruit, rolls, dessert. My daughter helped me turn a shipping box into a to-go container into which we could nestle each dish. We decorated the inside lid so that when it opened, it transformed into a pop-up hearth, complete with a shirt-box "fireplace" and tiny knit stocking ornaments over an orange tissue-paper "fire." This is what happens when your own children are outgrowing the need for you, when you feel your days as "Mom" dwindling, when you find out about a kid without her mom at Christmas and news of a bomb reaches the part of your brain that never stops thinking about all the different catastrophes that could befall anyone. You build, if not an actual shelter, a box of food. You let that surge of caretaking energy go where it can—if not into saving the world, into saving this one day, or at least this one meal, for this one pair of people.

When we saw Ava's car pull up in the driveway, I set a tray of hot chocolate and cookies on our back porch. She and her boyfriend waved and smiled as they walked down the backyard path to join us, cheerily introducing themselves as they settled side by side on seats near the fire. John and I sat across the porch. In hindsight, I realize we peppered them with questions exactly the way grown-ups are always, annoyingly, interrogating young people.

"What's your major?" "When do you graduate?" "Whatclassesareyoutaking, doyouliveoncampus, doyouhaveroommates, howsthefoodatschool?" They answered every question with enthusiasm, taking turns telling us about their aspirations to live abroad, to change the world, to go to grad school for one advanced degree and then another.

They sounded so young, but so self-assured. Had they gone home for the holidays, would their parents have heard this fledgling adulthood in their voices—or do parents hear their children as children longer than anyone else does?

When it was time to hand over their dinner box and send them on their way, I realized the food might get cold on their drive back to school and asked if they had any way to heat it up. Oh yes, Ava said, her campus apartment had a small kitchen. They could slide everything into the oven; it would be fine.

I stopped short of asking them to text me when they got back to school or check in the next day. I was not being called upon to keep mothering them past this moment, and there was no sense in trying to turn them into stand-ins for my own children. My own children were still right here.

"They seem like they'll be okay," I said to John as they pulled away.

ONE
LAST PART

STAY

For the past few years, my friend Petra and I have talked or texted on my birthday, but not about my birthday. We talk about Beth, our mutual friend who died. We laugh about how much we enjoyed Beth's hilarious, rambling emails, what an astute observer of human nature she was, how she adored stories of social awkwardness—both hearing others' and sharing hers. We rehash the latest celebrities-behaving-badly gossip and say, "She would love this."

We touch, briefly, on the memory of her death itself. We say, again, what a tremendous testament to love her final months were. We talk about how shitty and unfair it is that after all that love came loss, that everyone loving her wasn't enough to hold her here. Petra is younger than me by a few years, but we are both old enough to know that love isn't guaranteed to keep anyone safe—and we are both human enough to be mad about it.

I remember exactly where I was standing, next to my front door, when Petra called to tell me Beth had died. I paced around the living room rug. We didn't know what to say. Mostly we sniffled.

Petra, Beth, and I lived in three different cities

and knew one another from the book world. We were work friends, really, but I had become outside-of-work friends with them both in the past couple of years. Beth was someone I kept tabs on from afar, but not on a daily basis. If I'd made a list of people I needed to worry about most, I don't even know if I'd have thought to put Beth on it. I had known she was unwell, but I had no idea how sick she was. I thought things had taken an upturn. Or maybe I just wanted to think they had. Maybe I needed to think that because I didn't have the bandwidth to worry about her, too.

Deep down, I must not have really thought she was doing better, because when Petra told me what had happened I felt, instead of surprise, a kind of recognition. The news confirmed what I hadn't wanted to admit I feared.

I had a similar but slightly different sense of recognition when I saw my son on the floor that early morning: *Oh. There it is.* In his case, it wasn't that I hadn't made space to worry about him (I worried about the kids all the time); it's that the worry had finally materialized. This feeling is almost—not really, but almost—a kind of relief, because even if you don't want the awful thing to have happened, even if you'd give anything to rewind time and prevent it somehow, at least now that it has come, you can stop dreading it.

If only we knew which people we should be paying attention to, how wide the circle should be. And if only we were all allotted just one awful thing. Then, when it happened, we would know we didn't have to wait for any more. The problem with worry is that the scope is infinite.

I know people who downplay their birthdays—who say, "Don't you dare throw me a party," and mean it. I have never said that sentence. If you ever hear me say, "Don't throw me a birthday party," book me immediate surgery, because I definitely have a tumor pressing on the part of my head where my personality lives. *Always* throw me a birthday party. Hell, throw a party even if it's not my birthday. Throw a no-reason party.

I've had it explained to me by the no-party crowd that to some people, a birthday is a sad occasion. It means they are older and one year closer to dying. I get that. I've heard others say birthdays make them take stock of the past year and feel bad about all they failed to accomplish. I get that, too.

I love birthdays, and not just because my favorite coffee shop gives out free lattes. It's not about a childhood wish to have my name announced on the radio, although I want that, too. I want the whole restaurant to sing a song. Maybe with a live band? Good call. Turn the whole thing into a parade dedicated to celebrating the day of my birth? I would not stop you. But to be clear: I want this for everyone else, too. I want *you* to get the free coffee, and *your* name on the radio, and streamers in *your* kitchen, and applause every time you walk into a room just to mark the fact of *your* continued existence with the sound of clapping.

To be a person is to be a mortal. It is to be a death waiting to happen to a body. But it is also, until that moment comes, to be alive. I love the word *alive,* how it springs to action. It has real spark, like *afire, alight, afoot.* It's jaunty, It quickens and pops from stillness to breath. Listen:

Living.

Alive.

The two words mean the same, but I like the second one better.

What I really want is to go around saying, "Yay, we're *alive!*" to everyone, every day. But that's borderline obnoxious, not to mention inefficient. It's not an organized system. Birthdays are helpful for sorting out whom to say it to and when.

When I was growing up, my mother taught me I was not allowed to leave a birthday party without finding both the birthday child and the birthday child's mother and saying, "Thank you for having me." I remember my friends' childhood birthday parties now mostly as a frosting-smeared blur but with a few distinct micro-scenes intact—at skating rinks, in backyards, overnight in sleeping bags, dressed in purple sunglasses once at a "punk party." My mom came to pick me up after one particularly messy art-themed celebration, and when I hopped in the car covered in paint she asked not why I looked like I'd just wrestled a rainbow, but if I had said all my thank-yous. I had not, so she made me get out of the car and go back in to say them. The rule was not negotiable.

My birthday, to me, is a chance to say, "Thank you for having me," to the earth and everyone on it.

When my son was little, he went through a phase where he said "stay" instead of "live"—as in, "How long can a person stay without food and water?" or "I hope I stay for a hundred years." I never corrected it. It was like life was a party and he was just wondering about the curfew. When he asked, "How long do you think you'll stay?" I answered, "I hope we all stay a long time." Eventually, he stopped saying it. I don't remember the last time.

Right now, I can count the length of time he will stay—literally stay, sleeping and eating here in this house with us—in weeks. I can count how long his sister will stay in years, but only on three fingers.

Since he got into college, his departure has

become more real. We got an official letter in the mail and sent in the deposit. His incoming class has started to "meet" one another on social media. He has begun browsing the course catalog.

I am nervous. Will he have a kind roommate who takes the time to learn what to do in case of a seizure? Will he get enough sleep? Will the pharmacy there always stock his medicine? Will he remember, next year or in five years or twenty years after that, how one night, when he tasted pennies in his mouth and was afraid the lightning would crash again in his head, I slept on his floor? And will he remember, *My mom had a strange thing for sleeping on the floor* or *My mom did not want me to be alone in my fear?*

I don't expect my worrying to stop. But when I see how excited he is, I am excited, too. When I told him, back on our college tours, that I wanted him to find his own home, I was beginning to mean it—saying it out loud helped—but now, I really feel it. I want him to go, because he wants to go. This is right, this is good. It is time.

Days before Beth died, I visited the city where she lived. I had hoped to reach out and set up a coffee date, but this was a short work trip. Meetings kept getting crammed onto the calendar, and I ran out of hours to give away. I knew I would be back soon, so I told myself,

Next time, and went home. A week later, she was gone. She got so sick, she decided to leave this world. She died by suicide.

In made-up stories, you get a through line. Straight or curved or squiggly, it connects foreshadowing to ending. To paraphrase Anton Chekhov: Efficient storytelling requires that if you put a gun onstage in act one of a play, it must go off in act two. But real life doesn't always deliver on every promise, nor every threat. Not every gun onstage will go off. It's impossible to know which ones will and which ones won't.

Life can change in an instant, that's a fact. But life isn't changing only in those split seconds when it appears to change, when someone is there and then gone. It is changing in every instant. Sometimes we see the change happening; sometimes we don't. Sometimes everything about a life looks the same from the outside, but on the inside it has all been blown to bits and rearranged. And sometimes life is changing for people while you're not thinking about them at all, and you only find out afterward.

I grew from a child into the adult I am now while constantly looking and listening, filing information away as preparation and protection. Along the way, I built up such a store of knowledge that the knowledge itself became a burden. What do you do once you come to understand that loss is limitless, that it can strike anyone, anytime, anywhere?

You could spend your every waking and sleeping hour looking for all the hints and possibilities—trying to predict, after every explosion, when the next will happen. Waiting, waiting, waiting. I have done this. I suspect I will again from time to time.

But I have to remember: I am not holding any planes in the air with my mind. My worry may protect some people, sometimes, but it cannot—it was never meant to—protect everyone, always.

John and I talk sometimes about our combined inheritance of maladies, the various autoimmune syndromes and degenerative diseases that wind around our family trees like kudzu. We cross-reference the possibilities with our plans. Let's say we build that house—how many good years do we think we'd get in it before my heart stops or his memory evaporates? At least twenty, we say. That seems like a reasonable expectation. Thirty, sure. Forty? That's probably pushing it. And if one of us goes well before the other? Which of us will be able to kick around in a house alone, severed from the underpinning strength of our partnership? It's not like we get to choose.

"Maybe if we live out in the woods by ourselves, we'll get sick of each other," John says. "Do you think you would murder me?"

"Would you murder *me?*" I ask. We laugh.

Late one night as we lie in the dark, I try to explain to him why there are tears running from the corners of my eyes into my ears. I tell him I am having "the Nemo feeling." It's like I'm back in that movie theater and I'm drowning in the helplessness of wanting to save everyone I love and knowing I can't. I feel like I took on more than I could handle eventually losing.

John wonders if perhaps thinking about this is not a peaceful bedtime strategy.

I try to explain that I am obsessed with death because I am in love with life. I grieve in advance of loss—losses that will definitely happen, along with some that may not—because I recognize that what I have is so good. I don't mean to muck up the beauty of now with my tears about later, but I can't help it.

I'm sad because I'm so happy. See?

As of right now, as I place my pen next to my mug on the kitchen table, the medicine my son takes works very well. He lives a typical—no, not typical, very fortunate—almost-adult-man life. He will have more seizures, but it is within the realm of possibility that his seizures could remain few and far between. If that happens, it won't be because I loved him right and enough, at least not entirely. He did not start having seizures in the first place because I loved him wrong or not enough.

Beth didn't die because everyone around her failed to love her enough. Her family and friends loved her with all they had. Still, she died. It's not that the love didn't work. It's not that the love was wasted. It is never pointless to love someone.

My daughter is rehearsing for another play. She is thriving. My parents are healthy. My back still hurts, and I still eat Cheerios. Time has caught up with me, and I'm telling this story now in present tense. I'm still in it, not yet able to shape it from the future's perspective. I can't see how it is all part of whatever comes next, because I don't know what comes next. What I do know is that the stability of right now will not hold. It can't; it never does. I have no idea when I or someone I love will face another crisis—whether it will be sooner or later, if it will be something I can help with or not. There is so little I can control. Less than I ever thought.

Years ago, I started holding my breath, and I let myself believe I could exhale as soon as "the uncertain part" of life was over. I don't know when I thought that would be. As far as I can tell, the uncertain part is every second we're alive, until the last.

I wish we could all stay forever.

● ● ●

One day, if I am lucky, these years will turn into distant memories, filed away alongside my childhood. Some images will stay crisp and clear; others will be washed away by time. I will look back at today and notice things I can't see now. I might think, *I was so young then. So silly. So full of worry.*

Perhaps, if I get to be old, I will become wise. Then I might see in retrospect how the tension of forces I thought were pulling me in two directions—life and death; cheer and anxiety; body and mind; gaining and losing—were actually holding me in brief, miraculous balance. I won't waste time rehashing my every move, wondering how I "let" anything and everything happen. I will laugh at the hubris of ever thinking I had such power.

I may be awed by what I was able to do despite all I didn't know. I hope I will be proud that even though I could never find the answer to "How will everything turn out?" I still went to bed at night and woke up the next morning and filled a dish with fresh water for a turtle. I sat down to work for a few hours, then stood up and walked my dogs. I helped a friend write a letter, planted some seeds in my pots, washed the crumbs out of the kitchen rags, and hung them to dry. I scheduled a doctor's appointment for myself and a dinner with my husband. I sent a funny picture to my children and watched on a small rectangular screen as each of them responded from wherever they were. From afar, all this activity might have looked like hardly anything, barely the buzzing of a bee, but I will know that it was all ablaze with life.

I do these things for the same reason my dad went down into the bunker, the same reason my mom slept on the sofa by his chair, the same reason my daughter looked up the first-aid video, the same reason my son lay down on the floor and tried to coax our dog to eat. We take care of who we can and what we can, near and far, because that's the job. That is life.

It's true: There will always be threats lurking under the water where we play, danger hiding in the attic and rolling down the street on heavy wheels, unexpected explosions in our brains and our hearts and the sky. There will always be bombs, and we will never be able to save everyone we care about. To know that and to try anyway is to be fully alive. The closest thing to shelter we can offer one another is love, as deep and wide and in as many forms as we can give it.

Thank you for having me.

ACKNOWLEDGMENTS

I owe heartfelt thanks to this book's extended family—the Bomb Squad, if you will—including:

To Kristyn Benton at ICM, who is both a tireless advocate and a careful reader, as well as to Cat Shook, who provided calm and unfailing assistance time and again.

To Trish Todd—the woman, the legend, the book champion—as well as to the many hardworking, talented professionals at Atria Books and Simon & Schuster, including but definitely not limited to Libby McGuire, Lindsay Sagnette, Dana Trocker, Karlyn Hixson, Katelyn Phillips, Lisa Sciambra, Wendy Sheanin, Sean deLone, Falon Kirby, James Iacobelli, Sherry Wasserman, Erin Simpson, Emily Varga, Michelle Chung—plus every sales rep, all the marketing and publicity experts, and the teams at Simon Speakers and Simon Audio.

To Nicole Dewey and Beth Parker for wisdom, guidance, and endless energy.

To those who thoughtfully read the earliest pieces of this book, including Jennie Nash, Sarah Arnold, Sissy Gardner, and Molly Zakoor. And once again, to my writing group—Maria Browning, Susannah Felts, Carrington Fox, and Margaret Renkl—who donned parkas and masks and sat at awkward distances outdoors, but always showed up, week after week, even in a pandemic winter.

To the editors who first published some of these words in various publications, especially Roberta Zeff and Julie Beck.

To Heidi Ross and Kelly Kirby-Piovarcy, without whom my author photo would probably be a phone selfie taken in my car.

To more dear real-life friends than there is room to list here. (If we're on a group text and/or if I've had coffee or wine in your kitchen, I mean you.) Special thanks to those writer-friends with whom I've maxed out my calling and texting plan in the last year or two, particularly Anton DiSclafani, Dani Shapiro, KJ Dell'Antonia, Jessica Lahey, Lisa Damour, and Nancy Davis Kho.

To my former colleagues at Nashville Public Television, without whom I never would have had the opportunity to interview many of my literary heroes. Those conversations swirled in my head as I wrote this book and inspire me still.

To Ashley Van Buren for helping me navigate the delightfully strange world of theatrical permissions.

To readers everywhere, the independent bookstores that serve them so well—particularly my hometown hero-store, Parnassus Books (hi, Karen and Ann!)—and the booksellers who make it all happen.

Furthermore:

I so appreciate Garrett Graff's work in *Raven Rock: The Story of the US Government's Secret Plan to Save Itself—While the Rest of Us Die*, as well as what I learned on a tour of the declassified bunker at The Greenbrier in West Virginia.

Should readers want more information about epilepsy, including seizure first-aid resources, the Epilepsy Foundation (Epilepsy.com) and the Centers for Disease Control and Prevention (cdc.gov/epilepsy) offer excellent information and support. I hope it goes without saying that this book is not a medical text, I am not an epilepsy expert, and the experiences I have described here represent only my family's experiences, not anyone else's. Also: Not only do different people prefer different terminology in describing their conditions, but the language around epilepsy changes constantly as scientists come to understand it better. I thank readers in advance for their understanding if they encounter a term that differs from the terms they use or that has already evolved into another term by the time of publication.

I extend my never-ending thanks to the health-care professionals who have cared for my family over the years, especially James Keffer, MD; Katy Moretz, MD (who, conveniently, is also my sister-in-law, and who, along with my brother William, answered the phone at all hours during the events depicted in this book and at other times, too); and the staff of Monroe Carell Jr. Children's Hospital at Vanderbilt. My family and I are extraordinarily grateful for Cary Fu, MD, whom I know is just a human being but is also a superhero, at least to us.

I am so lucky to have parents, who, if they regret having a memoirist for a daughter, have been kind enough never to say so out loud, at least not to me.

Most of all, this book is for Team Philpott. John, my own personal bomb shelter, deserves credit for turning to me on the sofa one night and saying, "I hope you're writing all this down." Along with our children, he took the time to read and offer input on this material graciously and generously at multiple stages. Speaking of whom: My son and daughter, WC and MG, blow me away with their strength, humor, and kindness every day. I would throw myself on a grenade for all of you.

PREVIOUSLY PUBLISHED AND COPYRIGHT PERMISSIONS

Parts of the following essays, published by these outlets, appear in some form in this book:

New York Times
"Hard Knock Life: What Are the Turtles Telling Me?"
"The Great Fortune of Ordinary Sadness"
"This Togetherness Is Temporary"
"I'm So Excited for 40th Grade"
"For Those We Can't Always Protect"

Atlantic
"Face Hunger: What We Miss When We're Masked"

ABOUT THE AUTHOR

Mary Laura Philpott is the author of the national bestseller *I Miss You When I Blink*. Her writing has been featured frequently by the *New York Times* and also appears in such outlets as the *Washington Post*, the *Atlantic*, and *Real Simple*, among others. A former longtime bookseller, she also hosted an interview program on Nashville Public Television for several years. Mary Laura lives in Nashville, Tennessee, with her family.

Center Point Large Print
600 Brooks Road / PO Box 1
Thorndike, ME 04986-0001 USA

(207) 568-3717

US & Canada:
1 800 929-9108
www.centerpointlargeprint.com